I0256263

Change and Thrive

A Modern Approach to Change Leadership

CHANGE AND THRIVE

A Modern Approach to Change Leadership

Wendy L. Heckelman, Ph.D.

Copyright © 2020 by Wendy L. Heckelman, Ph.D.

Book Design by Kat Hargrave

All rights reserved. This book or any portion thereof may not be reproduced or used in any manner whatsoever without the express written permission of the publisher except for the use of brief quotations in a book review.

Printed in the United States of America

First Printing, 2020

ISBN 978-1-7344880-0-5 (hardcover)

Contents

Acknowledgements	1
Introduction: The Change Age	2
Chapter 1: Profile of a Transition Leader	9
Chapter 2: Welcome to the 5C's of Transition Leadership®: A Definitive Approach	20
Chapter 3: For the Love of Communication	22
Inside a Change Journey: Titanic Treatments	26
Chapter 4: Take Ownership of Change and Transition COMMIT	27
Chapter 5: Plan for Risk CONSTRUCT	42
Chapter 6: Lead Your Team Through Transition CREATE	53
Chapter 7: Coach Through Transition COACH	69
Chapter 8: Establish Metrics and Milestones CALIBRATE	81
Out of the Wild Now, Change! (Complete Your Transition Plan)	88
About the Author	97
References	99

Acknowledgements

It's a wild but wonderful experience to write a book. This one represents many years of work on a universal but often misunderstood topic: change leadership. Change is constant. Leadership is essential. Both are widely sliced and diced as subject matter worth reading about, but key figures made this book distinguished.

First, I must thank Sheryl Unger, who has worked alongside me for the last twenty years. She was instrumental in helping me shape the 5C's framework which has been the basis for a very successful practice that has profoundly helped dozens of clients. Sheryl has been a trusted and exceptional partner and without her, this book would not have been possible.

Thank you, Tianna Tye, for organizing and cheering on the very process of writing this book. You kept your eyes on the prize and did not waver, up-leveling the quality of content for the masses.

Thank you to my entire team at WLH—your knowledge, creative fuel, and dedication always remind me why I do what I do. You are the best group of professionals and I value each and every one of you!

Thank you to the many clients who I've had the privilege to serve over the last twenty-eight years. You are all the change agents of the future and the motivation for this book!

Thank you, Candi Cross, for bringing superb "beautifying" skills, spirited partnership and a few Sundays to this project.

Finally, whenever I think of my journey, I think of my tribe. Harris and Adam, we have been through a lot together and you are, without question, the light of my life. Skyla, you are the daughter I never had and my best friend. Adam, you are an amazing, committed partner and have helped me "see" and grow. Jolie, you are the path forward and I know you will become a fiercely independent and empowered woman. All of you are the heart of my soul!

INTRODUCTION

The Change Age

> "Your success in life isn't based on your ability to simply change. It is based on your ability to change faster than your competition, customers, and business."
>
> —Mark Sanborn

There is power and pain in change. Most importantly, there is continuity. And if you are fortunate enough to hit the jackpot, there is gratification and renewal. I have the privilege of working in the life sciences and pharmaceutical industry, and I frequently witness stunning transformations.

Remember that economic downturn in 2008-2010 that rocked the globe? Organizations had to swiftly endure change. They were downsizing, refocusing, and trying many different strategies to jump-start services and products.

Chartered Management Institute in the UK, with frequent contributor, Paul Arnold, describe the RBS Group turnaround as one of the greatest examples of change management in business history:

Following the 2008 financial crisis, RBS Group was ordered to sell its insurance business by European Union regulators, as a condition of RBS receiving billions of dollars in state aid. RBS's insurance business, led by Paul Geddes, was tasked with separating its operations from RBS Group into a standalone company, in order to be ready for either a trade sale to a competitor, or listing on the stock market.

Geddes and the insurance business's leadership at the time jumped into a large-scale change event action and turned the opportunity into a positive exercise, using the separation process to create a viable, standalone, rebranded insurance organization, now known as Direct Line Group. It took eighteen months to distinguish every single strand of the business, from customer data, to independent functions and governance.

The entire approach had to be one of controlled urgency—there was no plan B and the leadership teams embraced the need to shift their people on to the next step as rapidly and as efficiently as possible. Once the separation had been effected, the focus was on creating a new brand and rapidly building the business into a viable standalone operation.

Primer on Failure and Change Fitness

If you are a leader of teams, not just projects, you have a choice to make before any change engagement. Will you demonstrate strength not just internally but outwardly in order to get this type of initiative off the ground? Ownership of the responsibilities tied to such a holistic program is fundamental. Then, in order to improve, you must be willing to challenge your current circumstances. The very essence of change is that it can happen quickly, right before your eyes. Will you be ready for its significance?

The minute that you announce change is coming, everyone will shift in their seats with a range of emotions. Some of them will have had personal dealings with another transition leader and developed negative views concerning change. Others cooperated in the past and landed on successful results that still make them smile. Some had simply stayed clear of a transition leader in intimidation, with their nose to the grind, hoping they would never be called for a one-on-one. A handful didn't collaborate at all and they know it. Be ready for all of this "change baggage." As long as you are aware of this, your display of solidarity and transparent communication will be like a new coat of paint—fresh and interesting…but it may take time to get used to it.

Change is leading people on steroids! It is the extreme of leadership. Everybody will have their own issues they'll need to work through. If you are an inept leader to begin with, you'll certainly be a damaging leader through change. This book doesn't revolve around building and cultivating leadership, though there are natural pieces reminiscent of personal and professional development. With this caveat out of the way, you've arrived at these pages and are at least open to thriving through change.

Speed, Grit, Grace

We all get that "change is the new constant," but what does this really mean in the throes of an actual program to shift departments, strategy, service or product suite, and in some cases, entire infrastructure?

Based on my experience, one thing I will continue to press throughout *Change and Thrive* is that change agility is one of the critical components of leadership. At its core, change agility is the ability of a business to realize and sustain its full potential both in terms of its profits and its people, *regardless of* internal changes, such as interruptions to your supply chain, outdated IT systems, and being heavily reliant on one customer, or external environment changes: demographic, economic, political, ecological, socio-cultural, and technological forces.

Change agility delivers better competitive advantage, higher customer satisfaction and retention, increased employee productivity and retention, and faster time to work on new opportunities.

Recognizing that change agility is defined as "the ability to move with balance, speed, and flexibility to achieve a competitive advantage," consider yourself in the midst of your organization's current change. How would you perform on this drill?

1. *Balance.* Quick, subsequent change is known to knock leaders off-balance. How quick are you to understand and accept the case for change and make a personal commitment to be a change champion?
2. *Speed.* How quickly can you think and react to change and barriers that inevitably pop up during change implementation?
3. *Flexibility.* The most flexible organizations do not fight change. Don't wind up crying on the cutting room floor with your obsolete product or service!

Change agility is a skill that can be developed. As you move through *Change and Thrive*, keep the aforementioned dimensions of change agility in mind. Work to recognize and address any opportunities to improve your change agility as you go along.

The reality is that if you are not agile, you might as well go home. (Take my book with you!) The world will change a million times on you. The construct here is equipping somebody to discover for oneself and keep the business running. Pay attention to the business components. Change is not about a nice-to-have; it's a *must-have* if you want to survive.

Every organization is under constant pressure to keep pace with an endless changing marketplace. There are increasing rates of volatility, uncertainty and complexity driven by technological advances, globalization, geo-political instability, and shifting consumer demands. An organization must consider all of these factors when establishing and executing its strategy. More importantly, it needs to be responsive and adaptive no matter the size or make-up of the organization. Organizations that can adapt easily and manage change in a deliberate, well-planned manner using an approach like the one this book will guide you through, are most likely to enjoy success and longevity.

Today's organizational leadership needs to be skilled in large-scale, and sometimes ongoing, organizational transformations. However, the track record of companies succeeding at large-scale change is not impressive. Seventy percent of them fail!

Failure is defined by "lack of achieving strategy and desired results." Organizations fail for two reasons:

o *Lack of clearly defined implementation plans.* How do we go from A, to B, to C? Organizations don't necessarily do that on a granular level, and they don't practice the art of repeating the message. (It takes seven times to hear a message. One instance is not going to "get 'er done!")

o *Leaders do not possess the skills to lead others through transition.* This is the most glaring and damaging deficiency.

Unique, proprietary and results-driven, the methodology presented in *Change and Thrive* is focused on those two gaps.

In real terms, a failed change program translates to measurements where profits are not realized, return on investment is low, cost-saving synergies are not as expected, and other metrics of market share or competitive advantage change are not fully recognized. If you want a glimpse at the devastation, consider the gadget bloodbath of Motorola. Motorola invented the cell phone and dominated the global market in the mid-80s to early-90s. However, when digital technology emerged around 1994, AT&T requested a digital phone. Motorola stuck to their analog guns, allowing Nokia to step in and fulfill demand. Motorola, late to the digital game, found their market share drop to fewer than 14 percent by the early 2000s.

If it's not so obvious that you need to instigate change, you absolutely must see what changes are approaching, then react and respond.

Many leading business management experts and academic researchers have explored the factors that contribute to success or failure. Each study and after-action review sheds additional insight into what organizations must do to be part of the successful 30 percent. The change management models and lessons learned provide leaders with a multitude of ideas to incorporate into their change planning and execution efforts.

The 30 Percent Success Club

Organizations that are successful at change take a *whole systems approach*. Business management experts and consultants have provided various models and practical tips to ensure the organizational change efforts achieve success.

Common factors that differentiate success from failure are:

- Their leaders effectively address the impact of change at the organizational, team, and individual level. Specific implementation plans are designed and executed to address the impact of the change at all three levels.

- They identify the business risks most likely to jeopardize their business during the transition and take action to mitigate them. These risks and mitigation strategies are then communicated, with clear metrics, to alert others regarding problems.

- Their leaders, at all levels of the organization, are capable of leading others through the transition. Change agility is valued and a strategy is put in place to develop the associated skills with change management. Additionally, specific actions and guidance are included for leaders in the implementation cascade.

- They monitor progress against transition plans and recalibrate quickly to reach intended performance goals. Metrics for success are established and closely monitored. More importantly, leaders throughout the organization understand that recalibration is needed throughout the process.

- They place importance on constant and open communication. Leaders are provided with support when communicating the business case for change. They are held accountable for communicating with their manager, their peers, and their direct reports regarding the impact of change and their plans to address the challenges.

- Their leaders recognize that organizational culture must be shaped and can be either an accelerator for adopting change or an inhibitor to success. The organization includes specific actions related to culture change in the overall execution plan.

A recurring theme of the above listed factors is the role of the leader and the actions they take during the change efforts. Harvard professor and internationally renowned thought leader on change, John Kotter, acknowledges this gap, calling for greater emphasis on "change leadership," noting that "Almost nobody is very good at it."

Of particular importance is the preparation of middle-level and first-line managers to guide individuals and their teams through the transition and to execute against the change strategy. When done effectively, these managers don't just survive the change; they find a way to thrive during this change. Through their concerted efforts, the organization then excels and innovates. Based on research and validated through more than twenty-eight years of working with hundreds of clients, *Change and Thrive* directly applies to these managers and focuses on two of the primary needs associated with large-scale change:

o The need for effective implementation planning and execution excellence.

o The need to ready and prepare leaders to guide others through transition.

A framework referred to as the *5C's of Transition Leadership*® addresses both needs. This model helps the organization systematically design the implementation cascade while also preparing leaders to execute the change throughout the organization:

o COMMIT by owning the change and preparing to lead.

o CONSTRUCT a plan to address business impact and risks.

o CREATE a high-performing team to deliver results.

o COACH direct reports through the transition.

o CALIBRATE to ensure success.

Change and Thrive focuses on the leader and their role, as well as their related responsibilities. Chapter 1 further explores the role of the leader during large-scale change. Chapter 2 introduces the 5C's of Transition Leadership®, and then dedicated chapters explain each of the steps with supporting tools and checklists. We also go "Inside a Change Journey" to more poignantly mimic conversations (and escapades!) that occur as shown through our hard-working team of 150 senior leaders at "Titanic Treatments," an exemplary biotech company making waves in New York City's new biotech hub and around the world.

Since executing large-scale change is rarely a sequential process, and readers will be armed with different levels of experience, readers should ensure they navigate this book based on their unique needs.

Template for Transition: Your Plan

The fundamental goal of this book is to provide you with the information needed to create an implementation "roadmap" or "Transition Plan" that will help you prepare to successfully lead your team through a large-scale change effort. In order for you to *Change and Thrive*, ideally, you will have the ability to perform the following actions required to create a Transition Plan:

o Assess and address personal needs and gaps related to organizational change.

o Determine how the change impacts the business and make plans to ensure performance goals are met, while also addressing potential business risks.

o Translate the strategic change effort and take steps to create a high-performing team.

o Assess and coach each direct report's challenges and personal commitment to the organizational change.

o Establish metrics and milestones for success.

> "As we *Change and Thrive* throughout our personal and professional journeys, let's remember our uniqueness, aspire to greatness and focus on what is within our control. Let's also commit to communicating concerns, seeking counsel, and influencing others to take action on matters related to the change initiative."
>
> —*Wendy L. Heckelman, Ph.D.*

CHAPTER 1

Profile of a Transition Leader

"A leader takes people where they want to go. A great leader takes people where they don't necessarily want to go, but ought to be."

—Rosalynn Carter

Change? What change? Change is an event. It happens *outside* of us. It's usually tangible and concrete.

When it comes to organizations, the accumulating influence of the mega-trends has finally settled in. Those trends are: the rise of globalization, the expanding utility of data and information, and the increase in the speed of *everything*.

In turn, these trends have led to dramatic shifts in markets, in relationships with customers, and in the need for innovation. This has changed the dynamics of competition forever. Competition lurks in the crevices of every industry and waits to strike when the other guy is most vulnerable, and this is typically during an organizational shift or change program. After all, who's looking?

Is globalization so different than it was a few years ago? Yes! Capital now goes anywhere in the world that it's needed. The means of production have shifted to wherever costs are lowest. Trade barriers have been reduced almost everywhere. There are also billions of new consumers in the developing world. While this puts tremendous pressure on resources, the environment, and the ability of established businesses to deliver competitive value, humanity as a whole is more prosperous than it has ever been, and there are more opportunities for businesses to sell goods and services than ever before. The world has finally become a "global marketplace."

The dissemination of information has also matured. Communication and data transfer is instantaneous, but the platforms for exchanging, storing, and analyzing data continue to change. The shift to the cloud makes technology and physical location less important than content and ideas. As a result, organizations and their customers are dispersing and coming together in ways that are affecting how we work together, who we work with, who we sell to, and how we innovate. We now work from anywhere and buy from anywhere. We're also working and buying more intelligently because of the growing accessibility of big data as a powerful analytic tool. At the same time, social media has matured to become another powerful and disruptive force. It is increasingly difficult for organizations to control or direct their customers and critics. Instead, astute organizations are relearning how to interact and engage with those customers and critics, something that puts pressure on value propositions.

Finally, the speed of everything has also increased. Information and capital flows are instantaneous. Distribution systems have become incredibly sophisticated; Amazon, the current leader, can now deliver anything to your door the same day you order it. Work can occur 24/7. In addition, product life cycles have radically shortened. This last point has been an incredibly powerful disruptor. Whereas in the past, a product, technology, or service innovation might have afforded a business several years of profit and healthy space from competitors, today's innovations can be replicated so quickly that market leaders feel as though they are always under siege, and start-ups can become dominant players almost overnight.

Accordingly, organizations have seen their old markets change in sudden and unexpected ways, even as new and unanticipated markets are constantly appearing. Likewise, customers are becoming more available, more sophisticated, more demanding, and less loyal. Innovation and improvement has become a constant need, affording businesses no rest or respite. Indeed, competitors with the next disruptive innovation or process improvement quickly pounce on any complacency.

The endpoint of the megatrends I've just discussed is a wholesale change in the nature of competition. Only a few nostalgic years ago, "competition" seemed relatively straightforward and simple, even if the challenge of winning was intense. Today, organizations have no long-term certainty as to who their competitors and customers are or where their new competitors and customers are coming from, nor can they really be sure what goods or services they will be competing to provide. The bottom line is, change always churns its wheels. So, how do you deal with it?

In sync with teamwork, superb *transition leadership* is key. You won't go at it alone, but there are guiding principles to know about those you lead.

Uncertainty, rapid change, and the need for constant innovation has made work so complex and variable that individuals can no longer handle the load. No one person has the knowledge, experience, skills, or time to do the work that needs to be done. By way of analogy, consider the fact that in the past fifteen years every single Nobel Prize in science or economics has been won by a group of individuals, not a single individual. The multi-faceted nature of problem solving now exceeds the bounds of a single brain, even when supported by the incredible computing power available to us. The same is true inside organizations. Only a team can successfully keep all balls in the air at once. Organizations are recognizing how crucial it is to get top performance from all their teams.

In my work, I have also observed a marked increase in the overlap and integration between teams. In many ways, organizations are now comprised of complex webs of interlocking teams. The performance of one team impacts the performance of other teams, and the performance of the top team in particular cascades throughout the organization. Once, teams were semi-permanent entities or in existence for a substantial period of time, usually for the life of a specific project. Now, teams may have very brief life spans, or they may never physically meet, or they may include people from outside the organization, such as freelancers, vendors, customers, and others who engage with the team as insiders. Boundaries have changed. Rules have become less important than results.

The most important question during times of change is this: If teams take so much work, both in the formation stage and ongoing, is it possible to create and sustain strong, effective teams throughout the organization that are individually and collectively equipped for change?

The answer is, *yes*. But doing so requires the deliberate shift from an ad hoc, "play by feel" approach to team building and team management, to an approach based on simple but powerful principles of change management. This does not make team building and team management more complicated; it makes the process easier, more transparent, and more outcome-oriented. It does not take the magic, art, or personality out of teams; it provides teams with a structure and a system to make sure the magic can happen every time.

The best teams formed and led by change leaders are consistently excellent performers over a sustained period of time. A leader's engagement helps to ensure the most promising people are continually reaching their highest potential. The personality and attributes of the leader shape the culture of the team and become the channel through which success is achieved. The importance of the leader cannot be overstated, and accountability for under-performance ultimately falls on the leader's shoulders.

Without a plan, a proven formula, this gargantuan responsibility will swiftly break the back of any leader. However, over the course of my career and through working with hundreds of teams in transition, I can assure you that *Change and Thrive* is not only possible—it can be your passionate and achievable mission!

Principles of leadership are universal and malleable for every industry and type of organization. You can find outstanding leaders everywhere. But the change leader who employs a heavy emphasis on process just won't cut it; transition leaders take a people-centric approach and tap into the process that any human being goes through during times of change transition because it is an experiential spectrum, not a singular event.

Have you ever sat in a room with others and taken inventory of their leadership traits you might like to mirror?

For example, you may notice "Patricia," who had interviewed your best direct report and cut the red tape to shreds in the HR department in order to get her on-boarded in time to participate in very visible projects. On top of her multifaceted duties, Patricia is always the one to set a vision to maximize the organization's performance. She's acted expediently in tough times, making bold decisions in the face of obstacles and challenges. She demonstrated confidence and strength in her convictions and took calculated risks. And she championed diversity, creating and sustaining an inclusive and rewarding environment where diverse talent could thrive. She fought for equal and fair treatment and opportunity for all.

Then there's Stan, the middle manager keen on self-awareness, who came to you and actively sought feedback on his strengths and weaknesses. Out of all the team members on your last change team, Stan had shown the most excitement and engagement for maintaining a culture of improvement. He focused on raising the bar and set higher expectations for himself.

Then there was *Mr. Change* himself, Benny—wow, how dedicated he was to the pharma industry. He sure had a broad perspective of the business of caring for people. He pursued everything with energy, drive and a passion to win. He didn't give up in the face of resistance or setbacks. He was trustworthy and a skillful negotiator, who won concessions without damaging relationships. He could be influential, persuasive, and diplomatic without coming off as arrogant.

This model change team reinforces that every member counts for their individual contributions and group dynamics. If you want your change program to be successful, notice what traits they emit while applying the 5C's. Feel free to emulate positive traits! Celebrate the diversity of the collective.

Inspiration Correlates to Innovation

Implementing large-scale change and doing it well requires the involvement of leaders at all levels of an organization. At the top of the organization the senior leadership team is responsible for determining the overall strategic direction. These executives, if effective, create a shared vision for the change and agree on the strategic direction. At this juncture, it is important for leaders to clearly articulate the need for change and what the future state should look like. The vision must be inspirational while also communicating how the change addresses marketplace challenges, innovation, productivity, talent management, and overall profitability.

As part of outlining the overall change initiative, it is critical for senior leaders (the change sponsor) to focus on executing the change. In many cases, organizations will designate a change management team with a clear sponsor and cross-functional representation to design the overall change management initiative, including the execution planning efforts. However, as cited earlier, the failure to focus on implementation planning is one of the primary reasons change efforts fail.

This is when the leader or change sponsor needs to involve actual leaders at the business unit, team, or geographical level. These leaders will have the responsibility for executing the operational aspects of change on a local or smaller level. Typical operational matters may be the execution of a structural design change to the organization, implementation of revamped processes, or the introduction of new software. As they help implement the change, the leaders' role is to provide guidance to individual team members. This form of guidance is also referred to as "transition planning."

With your mind wrapped around successful implementation of the 5C's, remember that change and transition are as distinct from one another as black coffee and milk, and yet, they are conjoined. Here, we don't teach how to create a change. Life does that for us! Our *response* matters.

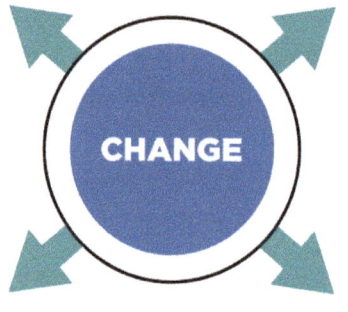 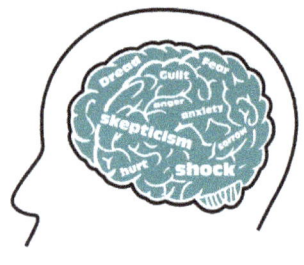

Change is an **event**, it happens outside of us. Usually **tangible and concrete**

Transition is our **response to the event**. It happens **inside** of us. Usually **intangible and different for each individual**

Transition planning is significant because the "people" side of the change effort is just as crucial as the operational side. Transition planning is not to be confused with change planning. Transition is our response to the event. It happens inside of us. It is usually intangible and different for each individual.

People are necessary when making operational changes occur and leaders play a critical role in helping the individual team members through their own transitions to ensure they can implement the changes. More often than not, organizations do not give this type of activity enough attention and resources.

It is important to note that leaders at all levels of an organization have a common need: Manage the impact of change on themselves first, then to their team collectively, and lastly, to their individual direct reports.

Different theories and frameworks have been proposed for understanding transition planning, but we will focus on two that simultaneously complement the 5C's and help leaders understand and manage the "people side of change." Both frameworks provide valuable insights for leaders who need to guide their teams through change now or in the future.

William Bridges' Transition Cycle

Over the past twenty years, an extensive body of work has emerged acknowledging the important role of emotions in the workplace, especially during times of change. One of the most influential concepts has been the *Transition Cycle* of William Bridges.

According to Bridges, when change occurs at work people often experience the same emotional responses they feel when major change takes place in their private lives (e.g., death, divorce, or relocation). Further, change causes people to react in complex, unpredictable, and sometimes contradictory ways.

The following table presents the level of acceptance and a sampling of emotions people frequently experience during times of major change. The experts who focus on individual reactions to change recognize that individuals often do not visibly demonstrate or express these emotions.

LEVEL OF ACCEPTANCE	TYPICAL FEELINGS
DENIAL	Denial, Shock, Confusion, Disappointment, Skepticism
RESISTANCE	Anger, Anxiety, Discomfort, Fear, Insecurity, Resignation, Sadness, Self-doubt
EXPLORATION	Curious, Creative, Unsure, Excited, Interested
COMMITMENT	Enthusiasm, Excitement, Trusting, Relief, Hopefulness, Engaged, Optimistic, Anxiety, Realization of Loss, Skepticism

The question becomes, "How does recognizing that these emotional responses and levels of acceptance are normal help leaders better manage change efforts?" Leaders need to be prepared to recognize and respond appropriately to each of these emotions. Even when the organizational change effort is clearly necessary and for the best, it is often perceived as a threat and can therefore, trigger emotions that are highly personal, sometimes negative, and may have an adverse impact on motivation and performance. In the early stages of any change effort, some people experience a state of denial and pessimism, which is "natural, normal, and a necessary part of dealing with change." For these individuals, it will be critical to give them "the opportunity to vent their frustrations, hostilities, or fears, which can actually assist them in accepting the change process."

Figure 1 shows the three stages or transitions that individuals go through. The complementary *Table 1* exhibits the types of issues or questions they may be dealing with at each of these stages.

FIGURE 1. BRIDGES' TRANSITION CYCLE

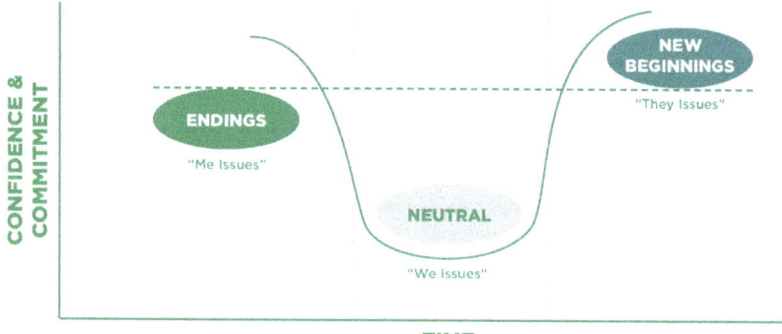

TABLE 1. TRANSITION ISSUES AND QUESTIONS

ME ISSUES	Will I continue to have a job?
	Will I have to learn new products and therapeutic areas?
	How will my job responsibilities change? My compensation and benefits?
	Will I be successful learning new skills?
	Will I like this new way of working?
	What happens if I don't?
	What new possibilities will this change create for me that didn't exist before?
	Can I reach my performance goals?
WE ISSUES	How will current customers be transitioned?
	How are we going to work together?
	Who will I have to coordinate with to get the job done?
	Why do we have to change as an organization?
	What are we changing into? Why does that matter to us as an organization?
	Who are we now? What do we believe?
	Where are we going? How are we going to get there?
	Can we trust and depend on each other? Can we get along?
	How will we know we're successful?
THEY ISSUES	Does leadership really support this change or is this just, "the flavor of the month?"
	How is our marketplace and competition changing?
	What do our stakeholders want and need from us?
	How do we meet those expectations?
	How much more change is coming our way?

Using Bridges for Transition Planning

Bridges' model is particularly useful for helping leaders understand the cycle of "emotions" that are most commonly related to change efforts and what needs to occur for individuals to emotionally transition through change.

I can't stress enough, do not deny that emotions are at play within any change. If change were only about *logic*, the 70 percent failure rate may shrink to 10 percent! And thank goodness for emotion, as feelings of excitement, anticipation, achievement, motivation, and inspiration all drive an individual's incessant need to fulfill goals, help their teams, and adhere to the organization's overall mission.

Based on this cycle, transition planning involves creating a plan for individuals to:

o Understand and accept the new reality.

o Prepare for how change will impact them.

o Know what will be expected of them in the future.

The goal of transition planning is to guide individuals out of the uncertainty and toward higher levels of confidence and commitment, as demonstrated in *Figure 1*. An important first step for team leaders is the ability to recognize where individuals are in this cycle. This will aid them and others through the transition:

o *Endings.* This first stage is marked by "Me Issues" in which employees' concerns about how the proposed change will impact them personally and professionally and what they may be losing in terms of control, status, relationships, and career potential. The "Endings" stage is often accompanied by denying that the change is necessary or that it will be "real" and lasting.

o *Neutral Zone.* This middle stage is marked by "We Issues." While people may have accepted the need for change, and perhaps its inevitability, they are uncertain about how to make it work and what's expected of them as individuals and teams.

- *New Beginnings.* Only at this final stage, after "Me Issues" and "We Issues" have been successfully addressed, are people able to look outside themselves to focus on performance as it relates to the organization's customers and stakeholders.

The sooner individuals can move through the cycle and accept the business case for the change strategy, the sooner they can focus on their individual role and performance. Even employees who embrace change immediately may experience corollary emotions that are decidedly unpleasant—in particular, the feeling of being overwhelmed. It is your role as a team leader to diagnose where individuals are in this cycle and accelerate their movement through the transition stages.

KEY TAKEAWAYS

- William Bridges' Transition Cycle complements the 5C's of Transition Leadership® and helps leaders understand and manage the people side of change.

- Leaders need to be prepared to recognize and respond appropriately to a variety of emotions.

- Excellent transition planning guides individuals out of uncertainty and toward higher levels of confidence and commitment.

CHAPTER 2

Welcome to the 5C's of Transition Leadership®: A Definitive Approach

"The task of the leader is to get their people from where they are to where they have not been."

—Henry Kissinger

Change will be a traumatic event for many people even though it may unlock the most marvelous results, reveal industry domination, or even start a revolution for your product or service. The structure of this change, however, will guarantee security that combats the unknown on the other side.

The 5C's of Transition Leadership® is deliberate as a structure in which to implement change and accounts for strategy, process, people, change, and coaching.

The 5C's of Transition Leadership® is based on the results of compiling various change management models and the research obtained from working on hundreds of client projects over the last two decades. The 5C's is a proven and practical framework for leaders consisting of five key activities required to lead others through transition during a major change effort. The framework focuses on the individual leader first, the business operational issues and risks second, and then the impact of change on the team and individual direct reports.

The framework consists of the following phases:

- **COMMIT** by owning the change and preparing to lead.
- **CONSTRUCT** a plan to address business impact and risks.
- **CREATE** a high-performing team to deliver results.
- **COACH** direct reports through the transition.
- **CALIBRATE** to ensure success.

Implementation of a large-scale change initiative is the centerpiece of the 5C's—not just the theory or anticipatory mindset of something to happen. The reality is that anticipation, which can abound in fluffy communications around a new project, does not equal *action*. The framework provides a common approach that all leaders in the organization can use during the implementation phase. This improves overall accountability for assessing unique needs and determining the actions required to achieve the desired results. Additionally, the framework addresses two of the primary reasons change efforts fail—lack of execution planning, and not providing leaders with the skills and tools necessary to prepare them to lead the change effort.

As a result of dedicating time and resources to introduce the 5C's of Transition Leadership® our clients have reported that this framework helped their leaders achieve the following:

- Communicate the business case for change.
- Build commitment to the strategic change initiative.
- Develop change leadership competencies throughout the organization.
- Address the unique challenges their teams face during times of change.
- Focus on individual differences in transition planning.
- Identify retention risks and engage in strategies to "re-recruit" first-class talent.
- Meet established metrics and milestones.

CHAPTER 3

For the Love of Communication

"If you want what you're saying heard, then take your time and say it so that the listener will actually hear it."

—*Dr. Maya Angelou*

In order for you to *Change and Thrive,* you will need to communicate often and in an impactful way. If we keep in mind that transition leadership directly translates the strategic change effort and takes steps to create a high-performing team, engagement, messaging and delivery will become ritualistic and embedded in your honorable, heroic role. And if you don't necessarily love communication as it stands, allow me to persuade you to at least become more attracted to its influence and power. You will be tasked in your transition plan to...well, "find the words" and reap the rewards. Think of your compliance with the following communication practices as a love letter to yourself, describing your stellar work when it's all said and done!

After all, communication is key to any type of relationship. It is also required for members of The 30 Percent Success Club. In fact, permanent members are master communicators.

If communication is not consistent, transparent, or on message, you lose trust, which is the vehicle for decisions, accountability and ultimately, progress toward your desired goals—in this case, a successful transition. *Trust me!*

Poor engagement plagues companies worldwide. In the U.S., a whopping 68 percent of employees are not engaged in their jobs, according to the 2019 Edelman Trust Barometer. This could be as a result of rampant communication issues between managers and employees.

Studies have also found that managers, not the organization, drive employee engagement and retention. Teams that have good managers are far more likely to be engaged and productive than teams run by mediocre or bad managers. Many companies rely on the quality of their product or service as their competitive advantage. Poor quality can sink a company. So, how do you get high-quality outcomes? It all starts with the team behind the product or service. If the team is not productive, properly communicating, and committed to quality and success, it's nearly impossible to have high-quality outcomes. The reality is that companies with strong leaders have twice the revenue growth of other companies. Without effective managers creating engaged and productive teams, many companies find their revenue stagnant or declining.

Communication plays an important role at all times during all activities. Senior leaders need to clearly communicate the business case for change and provide vehicles for employees to provide feedback and shape the change going forward. At the team leader level, constant communication with the team is central to overall success.

Open and clear communications are always a good business practice, but they are critical during times of change because they are the main vehicle for conveying the core messages of the change effort. Frequent and ongoing communications are needed to create common understanding, proactively address misconceptions, and sustain efforts.

Why, What, Who Can't Be a Mystery

Senior leaders need to develop communications on *why* the change is happening, *what* exactly is happening, and *who* is going to be affected and *how*. We call this the business case for change.

HubSpot, the global digital marketing automation company, has won multiple awards for its company culture. HubSpot co-founder and CTO Dharmesh Shah once published an article on his wiki page called (Ask Dharmesh Anything.) "HubSpotters" were enticed and followed up, engaging in a slew of discussions directly with their CTO. Shah also has over 280,000 followers on Twitter. In tandem, his blog, *Onstartups.com*, includes communication notes from the trenches of IT. He is effectively using a variety of communication tools to nurture relationships. With this kind of personal touch, I am going to guess that many employees would willingly follow him through a change journey.

Communications should include speaking points that will resonate, inspire, and mitigate potential concerns. Team leaders should use these speaking points to reinforce the change vision but also create additional customized messages for their teams.

Ongoing communication is critical for:

- Helping leaders to identify and address roadblocks, and take steps to correct any potential issues and recalibrate plans before things get too far off the rails.

- Allowing the organization to celebrate interim successes and share best practices. Small successes can help maintain momentum, and best practices help others see positive change results as realistically achievable. These things are especially critical given the long-term nature of large-scale change.

- Encouraging a pathway toward deep engagement, utilizing an empowering and dynamic communication process to increase team members' motivation and commitment.

- Constructing and expressing clear and concise messages in both written and spoken communication.

- Delivering messages that address the interests of the listener.

- Making verbal and nonverbal communication congruent to reinforce the intent of messages.

- Using reflecting, probing, supporting, and advising to demonstrate active listening to others.

- Providing the rationale for your feedback, whether to reinforce or improve performance.

In all of these somewhat utilitarian "corporate" techniques, remember that you can bring on an element of surprise and enticement in your communications at any time to balance out snags that are sure to come.

On that note, complaints are not to be double bagged and tossed in the biohazard waste can until they pile up for the crew to discard. Complaints are to be managed. But if you, as transition leader, remain enthusiastic, your case for change can be soundproof, even irresistible. It's true that tricky situations in the change program may demand confidence and a suggested solution on the spot, but a balance of formality and fluidity can ensure success.

Timeless Communication Practices

For all communications through your change program, ensure that you and your team follow the basic rules of great communication practices:

1. Be simple, clear, and specific to ensure that others cannot misconstrue what you write.

2. State facts, not opinions or emotions.

3. Show attention to detail by editing your work before sharing it with others. This will avoid simple mistakes.

4. Think before you write: For example, some topics are more appropriate for a phone conversation. Don't get sloppy or informal in your writing style for emails or texts because they are not "formal documents." Ask yourself who should receive the message. Don't copy the world and don't use email to share a company grievance or say anything that paints the company in a bad light, since what you write may be read by unintended and potentially unfriendly audiences.

KEY TAKEAWAYS

- Clearly communicate the business case for change and provide vehicles for employees to provide feedback and shape the change going forward.

- State facts, not opinions or emotions.

- Always keep the audience receiving your message in mind.

Inside a Change Journey: Titanic Treatments

Oh, look who has joined us! It must be time to get started on the 5C's of Transition Leadership. Instead of rolling out the red carpet, we're going to roll out something less glamorous yet more grand: a three-day leadership summit, where 150 senior leaders will be focused on change management implications and introducing a new geography and account planning process.

Titanic Treatments (a.k.a. TNT but only internally!), a biotech's commercial organization anticipating a robust pipeline, is scaling for growth. The senior-leader client wants to redesign the organization, knowing additional therapeutic areas are being added to the portfolio. In addition, the leader wants to build change leadership capabilities and ready their leaders to better execute change.

So, what do we know about Titanic Treatments and how successful they may be in their planning overhaul? We know that this brand is widely recognized for excelling at gaining market access through smart pricing strategies and boasting "beyond the pill" solutions for complementary business model innovations. With at least five major competitors shining a flashlight on their business model, scanning for a crack to expose, Titanic Treatments' polished reputation has been cultivated by medical technology and consumables, data and health info services, drugs, planning of management and care, and care delivery (a newly focused service). Culture is also unique here, with D & I (diversity and inclusion) embedded in its talent pool—so much so that the CEO has become an influencer with a few Tedx Talks, amassing tens of millions of views. And finally, the company has been chosen as a pilot for New York City's new biotech hub in an effort to become the top city in the commercialization of life sciences. In 2016, California and Massachusetts each counted about 30,000 biotech workers—about six times as many as New York. For the city that "never sleeps but always dreams," this won't do! The city's economic development arm is banking on Titanic Treatments.

With these positive conditions already established, we ultimately expect a successful transition. At stake: $20 billion of revenue.

But it won't be all roses and revenue for TNT. Remember all those emotions of denial and resistance (confusion, skepticism, fear, sadness, self-doubt) that may bubble up as either a result of a past bad change initiative or transition along their job history? Since this team is comprised of senior leaders, we may only have a few change first-timers; however, their energy will matter in the collective.

Be sure to follow their journey and learn how Titanic Treatments tackles each of the 5C's. Also, note how their communication techniques and tone may shift to align to their progress through the transition teachings.

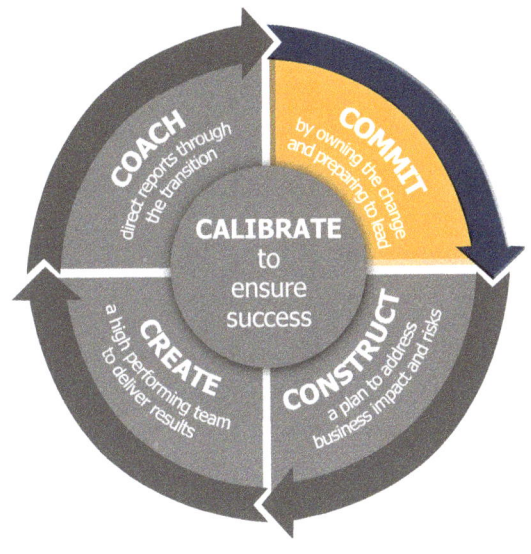

CHAPTER 4

Take Ownership of Change and Transition

"It is not the strongest or the most intelligent who will survive but those who can best manage change."

—*Charles Darwin*

Action
COMMIT by owning the change and preparing to lead.

The 30 Percent Success Club Quiz
Why must you evaluate your commitment and ability to lead?

Resistant Mindset
I can direct the change without buying into it.

Right Mindset
I am choosing my desired future outcome over my current reality.

Inside a Change Journey: COMMIT

In the first component of the 5C's, senior leaders need to get on board. They need to *Commit*. Since *Commit* establishes the correct psychological infrastructure, it may take time to cement it (and thus, the longer chapter to describe it!). The business case for change, which is paramount, requires explicit information on what is changing and the reasons behind it. *Commit* accounts for funneling this information properly.

Before anything can move forward, the challenges are laid out: picking different expertise in national and regional payers, integrated delivery networks, managed Medicaid, and long term care, as the company is already selling each of these channels. The massive change will be one person owning their geography. The knowledge of functional areas and knowledge of reporting relationships, and customer transition are all factors they are going to deal with.

For the team, the first step of *Commit* is to get offsite and spend the day together, and work through the *why, what,* and *how.* They are told the transition is driven by changes in the external environment, and it will represent a lot of "destruction"—destruction in what teams will call customers and the expectations in how they will work with these customers.

In spite of any foreboding around what destruction can signify (after all, this is TNT!), the individual leaders get on board and assess where they are in their ability to accept and lead through the transition. What they find is that although they have the pieces and parts to facilitate coaching and oversight, the personal issues are a different story. The leaders need to acquire additional knowledge so they can coach effectively. At the beginning of the initiative, they have been through so much other change they think it will be "same old, same old." In tandem, you always have a level of resistance with a leader because they think they know better.

But this morning, one of our designated transition leaders emphasizes, "Change starts with you! Your team will look to see if you are enthusiastic about the direction you are leading them and are thoroughly prepared to do so. Invest time in yourself upfront so that you are in the best possible position to lead your team."

With the stage set, everyone in the offsite session is taught to "*Commit* by owning the change and preparing to lead." The leaders recognize that change starts with the individual's acceptance and commitment to the new direction. In the *Commit* phase, leaders learn to:

o Manage personal reactions to change.

o Assess personal and leadership change readiness.

o Understand the business case for change.

o Prepare to lead: understand role requirements and implications.

o Close learning gaps.

o Align expectations.

Change is not successful unless people can buy into whatever that strategy and vision is. Commitment starts with the leader who is going to shepherd their teams through this change. Part of the mindset behind commitment is, *not only am I committed philosophically, but am I really on board with this? Can I understand how this translates to me?*

Go ahead and self-reflect. I would even argue that it is essential here.

Everybody has "me" issues. *It's all about me!* Well, if it is, ensure that you can answer the following questions: Do I know what I need to do as a result? How is my span of influence going to change? How is my focus going to change? Much like the leader goes through a journey in order to guide others, their direct report needs to go through their own journey: Can I *Commit* to it? Do I understand what it means to my role?

Commitment encircles the first phase of engaging anybody through the change process. You must work yourself through it, work your issues so you can be on board and ready to roll.

A promise of dedication can be a glossy premise—and it doesn't mean commitment at all. Commitment is in your gut, in your core belief. How will you get your team on board and through transition? While you adapt, you may also have to manage and coach people differently.

As noted by researchers, the primary and consistent factor to change management success lies in the role of the leader. Of particular importance is the leader's ability to inspire members of the organization to adopt changes that may seem threatening. If a leader somehow expresses doubt or demonstrates behavior that signals a lack of acceptance, then resistance is more commonplace. Therefore, if a leader embraces the change, provides a compelling vision, and takes action that demonstrates their commitment, others will take notice. Leaders need to face and manage their own doubts before they can concentrate on the transition issues of others. Therefore, to be viewed as credible and authentic by others, a leader must first deal with their own emotional reactions and level of commitment to strategic change.

TABLE 2. COMMITMENT SCALE

COMMITMENT	Agrees with the vision. Does everything expected and more.	*"You Can Count on Me No Matter What"*
FORMAL COMPLIANCE	Sees the general benefits of the vision. Does what is expected and more.	*"A Pretty Good Soldier"*
GRUDGING COMPLIANCE	Does not see the benefits of the vision. Does what is expected because they have to, but also lets it be known that they aren't really on board.	*"Whatever You Say Manager"*
NON-COMPLIANCE	Does not see the benefits of the vision and will not do what is expected.	*"I Won't Do It; You Can't Make Me"*
APATHY	Neither for or against the vision. No interest. No energy.	*"Is It Five O'clock Yet?"*

Carefully review this dynamic way to test your commitment with our 5C's "Commitment Scale."

The process that you go through to understand your individual emotional reaction to announced changes, willingness to accept the change, and ability to make commitments going forward should give proper insight into how others will also react to and accept change. Therefore, as you begin this journey, it is important to start with yourself as the leader, first.

The Big Announcement

As stated earlier, *Change and Thrive* **cannot capture** the countless business environments and scenarios that exist today. Imagine the power of an initial message about a major change coming. This could be a proposed acquisition, structural reorganization, systems/technological change, or a streamlined operation. Words and tone matter, as it will be the first blush of information your change crusaders will receive. What you implant in heads and hearts can make you the instant superhero or villain.

In some cases, people may have heard rumors; however, this *is* the official announcement. At this point, when a large-scale change initiative is announced, it becomes the leader's responsibility to accept and internalize the change goals and become a change catalyst for their team.

Once an announcement is made, individuals typically look to their direct manager's reactions to see how they should respond.

This is absolutely true, so never underestimate your impact. The team will pay close attention to what their leader says about the strategy and whether their actions demonstrate commitment to the change. The members will also evaluate if the communication is authentic and stated with conviction, as they will talk amongst themselves to gauge their leader's endorsement of the newly announced strategic direction. As the leader in this situation, it is important to start with yourself because *you* are the role model for your team. It will be more difficult for others to get on board if you have not fully accepted the strategic changes yourself.

Enduring Change and Other Emotional Displays

Before you can help others adopt the required behavior to achieve a large-scale change's objective, you must first manage your own initial personal reactions to change. What behaviors are you demonstrating? Are you in denial? Are you shocked and confused? Feelings of anxiety, anger, fear, and sadness over what is known and comfortable are typical behaviors of a "resistant" person. In addition, you may be resigned to the changes, yet unenthusiastically accepting of them.

As Bridges points out, it is important to acknowledge and accept where you are and move through these emotional reactions toward commitment.

Staying in denial or being resistant to change can hurt your effectiveness as a leader. Others will easily recognize if you are in denial or confused about the change. This may compromise your effectiveness and place a blockade in the way of helping others on your team accept, *Commit*, and manage their own personal transition with the change. Direct reports who observe denial or resistant behavior in their leaders will also be more likely to resist the change initiative themselves. You can help yourself achieve commitment and improve your own change agility by learning to shift your focus. This move would allow you to refocus on what may be lost as a consequence of change to the new possibilities that can result from the change. At this point, you can identify areas of uncertainty about the change and work to collect any additional information. If the information is unavailable, try to estimate when it will be, along with the source to assist you in your planning efforts.

Once the denial stage subsides, you can overcome the initial resistance through asking questions and exploring the ramifications of change. Getting answers can help you build your own level of confidence and commit to the change, especially if the answers to those questions include new opportunities made possible by the change.

Another common reaction is "change weariness." If your organization has been in a continuous state of flux with one major initiative following another, you may be guarded and slower to accept the business case. Again, be cautiously aware of how you are reacting, and be mindful of what you are demonstrating to your direct reports. Alternatively, take stock and reflect upon the changes of the past. Are there lessons learned from past efforts that you can incorporate into your current situation?

Confusion and anxiety ordinarily come from the recognition of an announced change and the fact that there will be new expectations and skills required to be successful. Further along in the chapter is specific guidance related to identifying any skill gaps and determining how to close these gaps.

During organizational change, many people experience personal stress. When changes are announced the workload usually increases. Typically, organizations expect their leaders to take on additional responsibilities and activities associated with the change initiative while still addressing other business goals. In this "do more with less" business environment, many individuals experience increased stress. All individuals react differently to stress. For some, they sleep less and become more agitated. Some eat more, while others forget or cannot eat at all. Either way, an individual's system is compromised and this can impact overall performance. Therefore, it is important to understand your reaction and ability to manage stress during times of change. How you manage stress has a lot to do with your overall mental, emotional, and physical health.

There are many suggested methods for handling stress, such as:

o Recognize your triggers and become willing to accept that you are experiencing stress. See if there is anything in your lifestyle that can be adjusted to reduce them.

o Act versus react. During times of change it is important to determine what is and is not within your control. Focus on what you can control.

o Take a deep breath; especially in the short-term to reduce anxiety or calm your temper. Over the longer term, use relaxation techniques such as yoga, meditation, or massage.

o Exercise is a great stress remedy and an effective means of taking care of "you."

- Practice time management to aid in the completion of essential tasks and establishing when to prioritize. Also include scheduling-focused time where interruptions can be kept to a minimum. (Remember that a change program will squeeze more time out of your day.)

- Watch your diet to avoid or limit things that strain your body's ability to cope with stress, i.e., limit alcohol, caffeine, sugar, fats, and tobacco usage. Eat a balance of fruits, vegetables, whole grains, and foods high in protein but low in fat for optimum health.

- Get enough rest and sleep.

- Talk with others about what is bothering you—friends, professional counselors, support groups, or relatives. If talking to work colleagues, ensure that you minimize complaining and make sure you are confiding in a trusted co-worker.

- Make some time for yourself. Read a book, watch a movie, play a game, listen to music, or anything else that you love to do. Concede occasionally; avoid quarrels whenever possible.

- Don't try to be perfect.

Presenting the Business Case

In Chapter 3, did I convince you to "love communication" a little more (or at least see the value in additional change-oriented chat that must be more frequent and effective)? I sincerely hope so! Nonetheless, it's worth reiterating here that to reach the final stages of Bridges' Transition Cycle, a leader needs to understand, commit to, and be able to convincingly communicate the business case for change to others. This is the rationale for change, or the "why" behind the change. Explaining the why may be more challenging when key decisions were made by others and the leader was not involved in the design of the overall change initiative. However, it is a leader's role to seek out the answers from their leaders and then possess the ability to further illustrate the company's core messages to their teams. If, for example, briefing decks have been supplied that outline the external market factors and internal rationale for the change, these should then be supplemented with evidence and examples from their own experience. To ensure credibility, it is critical that the leader explain the strategic drivers and rationale in their own words.

Seeking to understand the business rationale should not be an exercise in "spinning" the talking points. Instead, it should be an opportunity for leaders to share their unique perspective and to identify specific examples of how the strategic drivers impact their teams.

To help put the organization's talking points in your own words, you should be familiar with the various external and internal factors influencing your company that may be driving the change effort. External factors typically include global, societal, political, and demographic shifts that impact a given marketplace and eventually, buying decisions or business activities. Internal factors typically include efforts to reduce costs, increase efficiency, deal with leadership changes and challenges, and prepare the organization for the future. Use the following questions to make sure you are familiar with this rather large picture:

EXTERNAL FACTORS	INTERNAL FACTORS
What are the trends impacting your industry?	How does the organization need to adapt to remain competitive?
How are these factors actually impacting organizational results now?	What are a few key opportunities that can help improve the organization's effectiveness?
How does the organization need to change to remain competitive?	Do your administrative processes need to change?
What are the various challenges you are experiencing related to these trends?	Do you have inadequate resources?

When there is a clear understanding of the business rationale, there is a higher level of commitment. For you to be a change champion, you need the ability to communicate your own understanding of the business case for change in an authentic and sincere manner. This will ensure that you gain buy-in from teams and turn up the volume of enthusiasm.

Prepare to Lead: Understand the Requirements and Implications

Changes in strategic direction often necessitate a review of how work is done. Before you can help others through a transition, it is important to determine the implications to your own role. Consider how your role may be affected by the changes that result from a major organizational change initiative.

Role changes may be explicit, as in the case of organizational redesigns when leaders are typically provided newly issued job descriptions for themselves and their team members. In many cases, however, especially where change is happening at a breakneck pace, implications on roles are not fully known at the outset. Alternatively, it may take time for more formal updated job descriptions to be published.

We saw this point demonstrated recently when a large pharmaceutical company was changing their field sales organization's responsibilities. Initially, the role changes were not clear. Typically, their representatives focused on one or at most two products. The strategic change in direction resulted in sales representatives being required to sell a broader portfolio of products. This meant each representative needed to learn additional disease states and specific product knowledge. Not only did the strategic direction impact representatives, but it also impacted front-line managers and their coaching responsibilities. In all cases, individuals needed to be honest with themselves regarding what they knew, needed to learn, and how to effectively adapt to the added responsibilities. Although the organization developed group training to close gaps, each manager had to assess their own learning needs and include specific action in their transition plan.

When role changes are less explicit, it is your responsibility to determine if there are changes to goals, what must be accomplished, work activities, and how the work gets done. Other role implications include how you coordinate with others internally to accomplish job duties.

In a pharmaceutical company moving to a portfolio-selling model, you might find scenarios in which the individual sales representatives and sales managers need to change their call planning and interactions with healthcare providers. All need to increase their product knowledge and expertise in additional products and disease states. Having clarity around these changes provides individual managers with greater insight into what actions need to take place.

Establish a Personal Learning Plan to Close Gaps

When major change initiatives take place, a tremendous amount of learning is usually required on the part of all leaders. This could include:

o New strategies or areas of focus

o New customers or market segments

o New technology processes

o New leadership role with a new team

To avoid and prevent yourself from becoming overwhelmed by everything there is to learn, a formal learning plan should be developed that captures what needs to be learned, as well as to identify the best available resources. In the case of the pharma sales representatives, this step was critical in making sure anxiety surrounding the change didn't overshadow the benefits of moving to a portfolio-selling model.

The goal of this exercise is to reduce stress, not add additional burdens; therefore, focus your learning objectives on the short-term. It can also be helpful to keep longer-term career goals in mind and incorporate these into any development planning activities.

A key benefit of creating this formal learning plan is to keep you focused on what needs to happen for you to achieve success (especially in the short-term). It also provides the necessary structure to remain accountable to achieve desired results. Later, more guidance is provided on alignment with your direct manager on overall transition plans. Central to this is the identification and plan needed to close learning gaps.

··

Best Practices for Developing a Learning Plan

o Define what you need to learn by developing a set of focused questions related to performance, people, and processes. (*See worksheet in "Now, Change!" section.*)

o Identify any specific knowledge areas that must be closed.

o Determine resources available to close gaps.

o Create a structure for seeking answers to questions from internal subject matter experts within the organization.

··

One of the most dramatic changes that a leader can encounter is being placed in a new position and given a brand new team to manage. The leader needs to have the ability to juggle organizational and personal transitions simultaneously. To identify and track all needed planning and tasks, leaders should also develop a personal transition plan for the first thirty, sixty, and ninety days. This plan may need to include steps to acquire knowledge quickly about the organizational culture, team dynamics, and even technical/ functional knowledge. New leaders also need to establish and cultivate working relationships with new bosses, teams, and peers. Most importantly, leaders need to maintain personal equilibrium and not allow stressors to erode personal effectiveness and overall success.

Assemble Allies and Align

During the transition, each leader needs to align expectations with their own manager or supervisor. Investing time in this relationship is critical because your manager sets your performance expectations, interprets your actions for other key players, and controls access to needed resources. It will be essential to reach consensus on the critical challenges and priorities that must be addressed to ensure the change strategy is implemented successfully.

Think of this alignment effort as a process. There may be an initial discussion where the manager shares his expectations of you and checks in on your reactions. Subsequent discussions are often needed to further review and agree to your transition plan for yourself, the business, your team, and individual direct reports.

Proactive efforts to relay your plans demonstrate your initiative and willingness to be accountable for driving change within the organization:

1. Prepare for and schedule a conversation with your manager to align expectations.
2. Conduct meetings with your manager.
3. Keep your manager updated throughout the transition process.

Here are a few surefire tips:

DO!	DON'T!
Take 100% responsibility for making the relationship work.	Criticize the organization by criticizing the change effort.
Clarify mutual expectations early and often.	Stay away. Instead, reach out to your manager and get on your manager's calendar regularly.
Negotiate timelines to review your Transition Plan.	Surprise your manager. Report emerging problems early enough to make course corrections and avert negative consequences.
	Approach your manager with problems only. Include possible solutions, plans of action, and open issues to resolve.
Aim for early wins in areas that are important to your manager.	Run through a checklist at meetings.
	Try to change your manager.

Prior to any discussion with your manager, formulate your thoughts so you can be prepared to discuss your assessment of the business, review performance goals and expectations, share your team transition plan, and share your personal learning plan.

Make Personal Commitments: "Walk the Talk"

Organizational change takes place when a group of individuals accept, adopt, and make a commitment to execute the change and maintain the support of an organization's vision. You will know you are reaching the other end of Bridges' *Transition Cycle* when you have confidence in the knowledge and understanding of why the change is taking place. Consequently, you will feel more committed to the change. This section will help you solidify your personal commitment and provide you with the ability to demonstrate it to others—through your own individual behavior and actions.

Think about how you can convey your commitment. How can you walk the talk?

Demonstrate Trustworthiness

If you can remember back to when you learned to swim, or maybe observed others doing so, you've witnessed that crucial moment when the fledgling swimmer lets go of his instructor's grasp and sets out on his own. The hair-raising moment when the instructor assures the swimmer with the words, "Don't worry, I won't let you sink." That moment highlights the swimmer's trust in the instructor. That trust makes all the difference.

That same trust is crucial when people are experiencing the uncertainty of change. If they trust their leader, they are more likely to undertake a change, even if it terrifies them. The good news is that you can build trust; it only takes time.

In her book, *Dare to Lead*, Brené Brown outlines seven elements of trust to "brave," and I would concur that this anatomy of trust will surely elicit the level of loyalty needed for your team to weather change:

o *Boundaries*; mutual respect of boundaries

o *Reliability*: doing what you say you'll do

o *Accountability*; owning mistakes, apologizing and making amends

o *Vault*; not sharing others' information or experiences

o *Integrity*; choice of courage over comfort

o *Non-judgment*; feelings without judgment

o *Generosity*; generous interpretation of intentions, words, and actions of others

Model Consistent Behavior

Consider yourself on display as a leader. Expect people to be paying attention and observing your behavior closely, allowing *your* actions and reactions to *guide* their own actions. As people begin to better understand the new behaviors that are expected, it becomes doubly important for leaders to exhibit that behavior with absolute consistency.

You can make no stronger statement about your personal commitment to the change than to *visibly and dramatically* alter your own behavior to align with the change at hand. Showing enthusiasm, not resigned compliance, is critical. Negativism on your part legitimizes the negativism of your team—remember that it is human nature to mimic others' habits sometimes.

Your attitude and behavior are among the few things that are totally within your control, and taking control will result in favorable payoffs—positively influencing the performance of those you supervise and making your job as the leader a whole lot easier.

Suggested behaviors that demonstrate effective leadership during times of transition include the following:

- Be open-minded and practice good listening skills; seek to understand different points of view and perspectives.

- Suspend judgment and explore assumptions; welcome the opportunity to challenge the status quo.

- Use passionate, decisive, and engaging language; inspire confidence and commitment to a shared vision.

- Build coalitions that keep people focused in the face of ambiguity and conflict; discover common ground ("what can be done").

- Find creative, "win-win" solutions.

- Own up when things go wrong.

- Find innovative methods to get past apparent obstacles and roadblocks; create "I will" commitments and "we can" goals.

Call and Response: Rally by Repeating Symbols and Phrases

Another way to build support as the transition leader is to find a symbol or a few memorable, catchy phrases that convey the vision and rally support for the change. "Set expectations, spark magic." "Happy change, happy customers." "Invest in change, invest in yourself." Yes, you must be a zealous cheerleader!

Repeat the phrases and display the symbols and your teams will begin to do so too. Over time, this gives the change reality and legitimacy. Legitimacy directly counters any watery or paper-thin notion of change coming. Your team will get the sense of substance the change holds.

One of the enduring strengths of the quality movement remains its capacity to induce large numbers of people to adopt its vocabulary. Terms like "continuous improvement" have come to embody the vision and concepts that the movement strives to achieve.

As a leader, you should take the time to *Commit* to the beliefs, behaviors, and results you wish to achieve. By "walking the talk" you will successfully model the commitment to change that you want to inspire in your team.

Now, Change!
Critical Actions to Commit by Owning the Change and Preparing to Lead

☐ Manage your personal reactions to change.

☐ Understand and commit to the business case for change.

☐ Prepare to lead: understand the requirements and implications to your role.

☐ Establish a personal learning plan to close any gaps.

☐ Align expectations with your manager.

☐ Make personal commitments on how you will "walk the talk" to model the beliefs and behaviors that demonstrate acceptance and commitment to the vision.

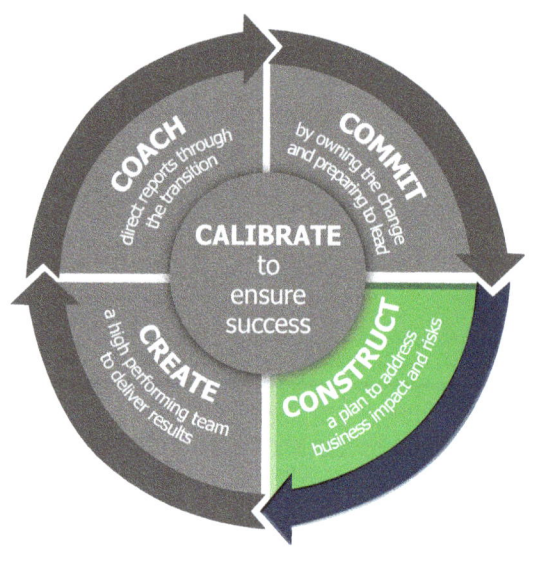

CHAPTER 5

Plan for Risk

"Risk is a function of how poorly a strategy will perform if the 'wrong' scenario occurs."

—Michael Porter

Action
CONSTRUCT a plan to address business impact and risks.

The 30 Percent Success Club Quiz
What are you doing to identify opportunities and minimize risks?

Resistant Mindset
If I focus on risk, I focus on the negative.

Right Mindset
I should determine areas of potential business risk that may be associated with the proposed change.

Inside a Change Journey: CONSTRUCT

Our Titanic Treatments' team is being tested. They're learning about risks, with an overarching question to think about: What are the business risks of change implementation and what are the strategies to mitigate those risks?

Carefully examining all the faces in the airy, sunny work lounge at the chateau, our charismatic transition leader quips, "If *Construct* were a witty talking head like mine, it would say, 'Hey, you're going through fundamental change, my fellow TNT explosives! We're going to have landmines all over the place. On a more conventional note, what do those risks look like? 'I'm going through this change process, but I better keep the wheels on the car and the car running while we go through this.'"

They have been through change in which an organization announced the change but did not give tangible ways to think about its implications.

It's about that time for questions and comments: "How do we keep customers during the transition?" "Are we hiring additional staff?" "You are asking professionals to acquire new knowledge and you're fundamentally changing the way you interact with those customers from an account based selling approach."

Together, the team spells out what they think are the most important risks and strategies for mitigating the risks. "Mary" learns she will have a lot of customer transition and customers in a new segment. She's relieved to know that there is a customer transition process and tools available for just that. "Jerome" must hone his ability in a new therapeutic area and receives a specific training plan. He doesn't have to go fish for the material himself. With this fundamental change, the company's Human Resources and training departments have all come to the party to support the change. The leaders have all identified the most important business continuity requirements to communicate to their teams. In addition, they have identified risks within their control and established a set of mitigation strategies.

A central component of *Construct* is, everybody will go through change, and there are risks associated with all the unfamiliar movement and may impact how somebody is able to adapt. For example, my firm, WLH Consulting helped a client conduct a transition for a massive expansion. Individuals sold cardiovascular drugs, but suddenly, they're going to sell respiratory drugs, requiring new knowledge and protocols for different customers.

The role of activities surrounding *Construct* is to identify mission-critical business requirements that need to happen *and* examine the most probable risks that will take you down through this evolution. Figure out what those mitigation strategies look like. As you review them, fearlessly think through the risks (after all, they haven't manifested!). Don't just be a cheerleader for a shiny, red strategy or vision. Be sure to back it up with explicit actions. Where do you stand in your readiness? Ask yourself this along the way. It doesn't have to be a perfect answer or the delusional feeling of being a model leader. It could be *will set, skill set,* or *mindset.*

Construct signals that you should realize the value of this change from a strategic perspective. What will take you down? What will have you stumble and break your toe or foot? Leaders need to think about that ahead of time. Again, one reason that 70 percent of companies fail to meet their change objectives is because they do not adequately anticipate and plan to mitigate business risks associated with their changes.

Every change initiative is different and each one has its own unique set of challenges or business risks that could cause failure. For example, "Mary's" customers will be impacted in revenue, market share, and other important performance metrics for both the short- and long-term. In other scenarios, there may be impacts to production, process flow, information exchange, and countless other areas. In almost all cases, the impact of the change disrupts the status quo and often leads to distractions among the team. When implementing important new initiatives, the leader must be mindful to ensure that business continuity is maintained and not compromised. Are you and your team staying focused on current goals and customer needs? Lastly, change impacts individuals. What are the risks associated with individual productivity, employee engagement, and overall talent retention?

It is also imperative to understand which risks a leader has control over and those that they do not have control over. *News flash!* At the team-leader level, you may not have control over all risks. However, it is important that you focus on the risks in which you do have control.

You can increase your chances of being part of the prestigious 30 Percent Success Club of transition leaders if you take the time to identify and understand the business risks that your company and team will face, work to prioritize them, and then create plans to control or mitigate them.

Maintenance and Mastery

Every business harbors ongoing requirements and day-to-day activities that require attention and maintenance. Any large-scale organizational change is likely to cause disruptions to these business activities. As a leader, it will be important for you to identify these requirements and maintain focus on current business performance requirements, while also planning for the upcoming changes.

The first step to address business risks associated with an organizational change is the identification of pre-existing business objectives (near to mid-term) that will be affected by the changes, as well as determining what adjustments need to be made to ensure success. There will be three business requirement categories:

o Requirements that are completely unaffected by the change and still need to be met, per the original timelines and methods.

o Requirements that still need to be met. However, due to the proposed changes, adjustments will be necessary to determine how or when they can be met.

o Requirements that no longer need to be met.

One of the most glaring risks when implementing change is the potential impact to customers, especially in the short-term. Since maintaining customer relationships is an ongoing activity, it is essential to assess what actions are required to reduce any business interruption. For example, during an organizational restructuring, the sales force's geographical and customer alignments might be changed. To preserve customer relationships and ensure a seamless transition, it is important to develop an appropriate knowledge transfer and plan of action. It is also imperative to determine if specific communications to customers are required and who is responsible for these communications.

A Forecaster's Mindset

In any strategic transition, inherent risks could determine its success or failure. Risk is not something to run from. It must be met head-on. Various types of business risk have a potential impact on an organization's overall revenue, costs, profitability, legal liability, and customer relationships. Ideally, the effort of identifying business risks should start with senior leaders scanning the organization to recognize the risks that all groups are likely to face and then share these factors with group and team leaders. If this is accomplished, your role will be to determine if and how these risks apply to your individual areas of responsibility.

For the risks that are unique to your own group, team, or geography it is important for you to take responsibility in identifying them. Remember, senior leaders may not be aware of or have the expertise to deal with these risks.

If senior leadership did not explicitly identify potential risks to be mindful of when implementing the change initiative, you should think about, identify, and take action to mitigate potential risks. Not every risk factor will be predicable. Some may not be within your control. However, it will be in your best interest to identify as many risks as you can and attempt to address or communicate them to others.

It is helpful to think of the risks as *external* and *internal* to the organization. Oftentimes, much attention is paid to internal change-related activities and leaders lose sight of external customer and marketplace-related business challenges. Here are a few considerations to help you identify potential risks associated with external and internal factors:

EXTERNAL FACTORS	INTERNAL FACTORS
• Marketplace and Competition	• People in the Organization
• Customers	• Incentives and Compensation
• Regulatory and Policy Vendors and Consultants	• Cross-Functional Stakeholders
	• Policies and Procedures
	• Systems and Technology
	• Change Implementation
	• Culture Change

Note that the last two business risk categories (implementation and culture change) are critical to change success, yet they are not commonly given enough attention. Large-scale change execution takes careful planning with continued effort to ensure that changes are understood, adopted, and sustained. It is important to identify and address implementation risks specific to the overall change initiative.

Are there issues related to timing, sequencing, and involving the right people at the right time?

There is great value in addressing existing culture and where there may be room for nuances or adjustments. An individual's beliefs about change will heavily influence their acceptance or resistance to the change. Companies that ignore these risks and try to "force" a change, either by trying to move too quickly or with heavy-handed "do-it-or-else" communication, could conceivably encounter employee resistance so strong that the change efforts usually flounder and fail.

Individuals should be rewarded for demonstrating commitment to the new cultural beliefs.

DISCOVERY SESSION: BUSINESS RISK

BUSINESS RISKS	KEY QUESTIONS TO CONSIDER
EXTERNAL MARKETPLACE AND COMPETITION	• Where is the business likely to encounter the stiffest competition in the coming years and will the changes hamper the company's ability to remain competitive? • Could the change initiative create any other barriers to respond effectively to marketplace changes? • How will the competition react and position themselves as a result of changes within your organization?
CUSTOMER RELATIONSHIPS	• Are the changes going to affect how, when, or with whom your team members interact with customers? • Are you changing anything about your goods or services? Does this need to be communicated? • Is your delivery method, timing, or style changing? • Are policies and practices related to ordering, payment, or general customer service changing? Will this need to be communicated? Where will extra attention be needed to ensure ease of operation and excellent customer service?
YOUR PEOPLE	• Changes to how work is performed • Changes that will require new knowledge and skill acquisition • Changes in how people will be measured and assessed, thus requiring updates to the Performance Management process • Changes that could affect employee morale and engagement • Changes in organizational structure that alter reporting relationships and team configurations • Changes that could cause individuals to feel "change weary" because they have made too many changes over a short period of time or have gone through a series of major changes • Changes in the resources that your team will be required to work with and function effectively. Do they have these resources or can they readily access them?

BUSINESS RISKS	KEY QUESTIONS TO CONSIDER
INCENTIVES AND COMPENSATION	• What behaviors are reinforced through current performance management measures, compensation, reward structures, and other metrics? Do these measures align with the goals set out in the change effort? • Are any procedures, systems, or informal norms likely to penalize individuals for supporting the change efforts? • What formal reward processes need to be updated? • How can you informally acknowledge and reward individuals on your team for adapting to the change and taking action?
INTERNAL STAKEHOLDERS	• For internal customers, how will these changes affect your interactions or interdependencies with other individuals or groups? • Will you have the ability to continue receiving and delivering what is required to meet business goals? • Are there new stakeholders you will need to meet with, depend on for deliverables, or communicate with?
POLICIES AND PROCEDURES	• Which existing policies and procedures could be impacted by the changes? Are there any that will need to be changed? How quickly do they need to be revised and what approvals are needed? • Do you need to check with individuals in your legal or compliance departments regarding the policy implications of the changes? • How will the change(s) impact decision-making? • Will the changes in policy necessitate changes in procedure? • If any procedures need to be revised, are any other groups involved in the process or dependent on the deliverables? How should they be informed / involved? • What staffing changes may be necessary to implement the new policies and procedures? • How will changes to policy and procedure impact any short-term and ongoing training efforts?

BUSINESS RISKS	KEY QUESTIONS TO CONSIDER
SYSTEMS	• What technical systems (e.g., hardware and/or software) does your team use and how is this usage impacted by the proposed changes? • Will existing hardware and/or software systems support the organizational change? If not, can they be changed quickly enough to accommodate business requirements? • What are some of the interim solutions available while the full-scale system changes are being implemented? • What are the risks associated with data integration and overall data integrity?
IMPLEMENTATION	• Will any work processes need to be temporarily terminated during the changes and how long will these interruptions last? • Are there existing or new deadlines that the changes will impact? • Are the right people involved and at the right time? • Will your group or others you will be closely working with go through the changes at the same time? How will this impact your ability to work together? • What other business priorities might cause stakeholders to shift attention away from, or even withdraw support from the change initiative? • What ripple effects could occur as a consequence of the changes? Look at your own group as well as others that you interact with. • What other land mines could exist for change implementation that would push efforts off track?
CULTURAL CHANGE	• Is there a simple, compelling vision for why the change is needed? • Have efforts been made to create buy-in for the change effort? Are they being well-received? • Are leaders modeling the changes they are asking others to make? • Are there existing beliefs or practices that are not aligned with the change effort?

Risks Are Priorities, Too!

Using the Business Risk Categories previously identified, as well as knowledge of your team and organization, and the prescribed change goals, develop a comprehensive list of business risks you are likely to face. When generating this initial list, do not worry about its length or whether the risks are under the control of your team. Once the list is generated, use the following questions to help you categorize and prioritize the risks: Which of these risks will your team have little or no ability to address? Which are the highest priority risks that your team should address?

Next, identify which risks are likely to have the greatest impact and which of those you are likely to be more or less successful at addressing. If you are a team leader, some risks, especially implementation and cultural change risks, may not be completely under your control. However, it is important for these factors to be identified and addressed at the appropriate level. You should inform change leaders/champions if you see evidence of organization-wide resistance, or issues likely to affect another team or group.

Another risk area that is within your control relates to retaining talent. When large-scale change is taking place and a lot of internal confusion exists, there is a likelihood of top talent becoming frustrated and looking to leave the organization.

This list should be validated with others including your team members, peers, manager, or other leaders. If possible, obtain broad input to ensure accuracy and completeness. Share with your team members and other internal stakeholders that your group interacts with frequently. As suggested above, leaders who appear to be championing the change within the company may also be good sources of information about what business risks your team is likely to face.

Coveting Customers—Mitigation Strategies

Prior sections were aimed at helping you identify the business risks that may accompany the proposed changes. In this section, you will bring these together and develop plans to address anticipated risks and minimize customer (both internal and external) impact. Think about your highest-priority business risks and affected customers. For each of these risks you want to ensure you identify specific actions your team should take to address them. Specifically, you are determining who will be responsible for doing what and by when.

Share with your entire team, if feasible, and with input from as many other key stakeholders as possible. Here are general rules to follow:

- There may be specific individuals currently in charge of sending communications regarding the change effort, either internally or externally. Check with your manager to determine existing efforts and ensure consistency of language with any prior communications.
- Training is a common solution to business knowledge and skill gaps, but if the organizational change involves layoffs, role changes, or forming new teams ensure that the transfer occurs to retain critical knowledge and information.
- Consider including key customers/stakeholders in your risk mitigation planning.
- Identify which customers may be impacted by the proposed change.
- If appropriate, ask customers to meet with you to discuss the upcoming changes and to ensure the company is continuing to meet their needs.
- Think about how you can be proactive. What specific data and perceptions could be monitored to "stay ahead" of risks?

Construct prompts you to acknowledge and accommodate risks. Remember that you can't avoid exposure to risk; you can increase acceptance and exploit risk in your transition planning.

Now, Change!
Critical Actions to Construct a Plan to Mitigate Risks

☐ Identify continuing business requirements and goals that need to be managed during the transition.

☐ Determine areas of potential business risk that may be associated with the proposed change(s).

☐ Develop mitigation strategies to address risk factors and minimize customer impact.

☐ Communicate and align with others on the risk mitigation plans.

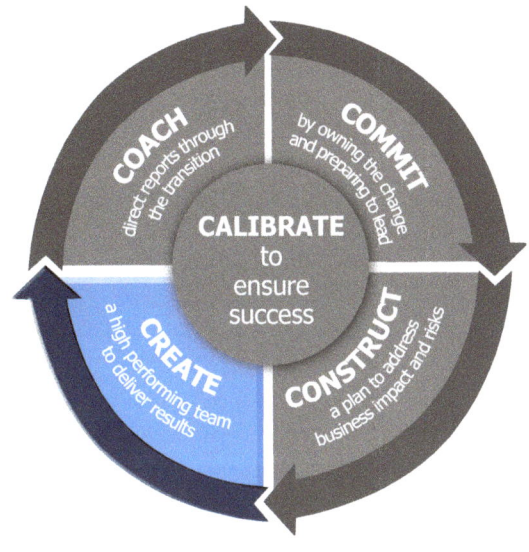

CHAPTER 6

Lead Your Team Through Transition

"Teamwork is the ability to work together toward a common vision, the ability to direct individual accomplishments toward organizational objectives. It is the fuel that allows common people to attain uncommon results."

—Andrew Carnegie

Action
CREATE a high-performing team to deliver results.

The 30 Percent Success Club Quiz
Why is it important for you to *Create* a high-performing team to deliver results?

Resistant Mindset
I don't have to focus on my team's transition!

Right Mindset
I will formulate my vision and expectations, and revisit goals, team roles, coordination and metrics.

Inside a Change Journey: CREATE

Our change team in-progress has come with certain assumptions. Based on their previous experiences, some team members think the company needs an entirely different team for change and this is not the case at all. With Titanic Treatments, the leaders are equipping them with the resources they need—not identifying other team members.

In many cases, the team won't change all that much. What's changing is the fundamental strategy, expectations in how to go to market and whom they will work with.

How do you as an individual leader get your team up and running in the first ninety days? Communicating strategy and clarifying roles is critical!

The softer side of change is working with leaders to equip them to make sure the team has roles, responsibilities, and rules of engagement across, up, and down the organization. Some leaders do not naturally gravitate to "soft" anything. In pharma, you can have three or four or eight people working on a particular account or customer. At the same time, team success means cohesion and engagement.

Rules of engagement are critical! And this team is quickly learning to get on the same change page by focusing on how to get through the change process together, replacing individual self-absorption with the prospect of team success in serving the organization's goals. Leaders have also committed to team jump starts, knowing there is a need to confirm roles, responsibilities, and ways of working, and ultimately developing 90-day action plans.

When you go through a change, you will have to decipher as a leader if the team is new or the same, but with a different focus. Any of those pieces and parts shift into what they should be for greatness, but *Create* underscores how you immerse your team and jump start out of the gate, and then find ways to work effectively together. This is highly variable.

If your team is intact, you are intact as a leader, and the focus is on strategy being different or the way you work with customers, you're focusing on that piece of it. When you have a leader or new team member, *Create* also encompasses getting strategically focused on chartering your team with rules of engagement, so you can move to high performance quickly. Teams cannot remain in obscurity for one day upon the big announcement of the almighty change!

With one client, WLH jump started forty-two teams upon a merger. We facilitated forty-two one-day workshops where leaders would set their strategy and vision, assess their teams' level of commitment, build action teams and rules of engagement. The cornerstone to every activity was "honoring" the teams as a collective of individuals with complementary skills.

The challenge of producing results is increased and intensified during times of organizational change. The team can easily become distracted, drop the ball on important ongoing business needs, or take too long to produce results. The job of an effective transition leader is to build a great team that works together to help each other win, especially during times of change.

Large-scale change can also vary in its impact on a team. The effects may result in staffing changes where people are assigned to new teams or if a new leader is being appointed. Internally, they could result in team members needing to interact with new or different stakeholders.

Externally, they could result in new customers, new alliances, new assigned geographies, or other variables. It does not matter if the disruption is large or small, or if the team membership is newly configured or remains the same. In any circumstance, team members must quickly understand each other and how they will work together to achieve their stated goals and mission.

In an organization, there are many types of teams. They can vary in size, structure, and longevity. For example, there are transient teams, i.e., cross-functional or task forces that are pulled together to address a specific issue or business challenge.

There are also varying reporting relationships, i.e., an account team where the leader has responsibility for a particular customer account yet their members may report to other managers. This type of team requires a leader who can influence without authority.

It is your responsibility to *Create* an environment where team members learn from each other and work together with one common purpose. Your role is to galvanize the team under a shared vision and help the team produce results. During times of transition, there is always much to do with limited time to do so. To help the team buy-in to the change, you must focus on what they must do, and work collectively to meet performance expectations.

Be aware that creating high-performing teams during times of change requires different types of activities. As in any leadership role, there is work that you must do on your own. At this point, think through various considerations related to the team's readiness for change and how the team needs to work together going forward. Once you put together a plan of action, there is a definitive set of activities for you to perform with your team. This includes conducting a team "jump-start" to gain a shared vision and clarify expectations. Finally, there are ongoing activities to involve your team in to keep them engaged, provide direction, and support efforts to implement the change initiative.

Figure 2 highlights five important characteristics of high-performing teams. As you assess your team, look for ways to strengthen each of these areas:

FIGURE 2. CHARACTERISTICS OF HIGH-PERFORMING TEAMS (SOURCE: PATRICK LENCIONI)

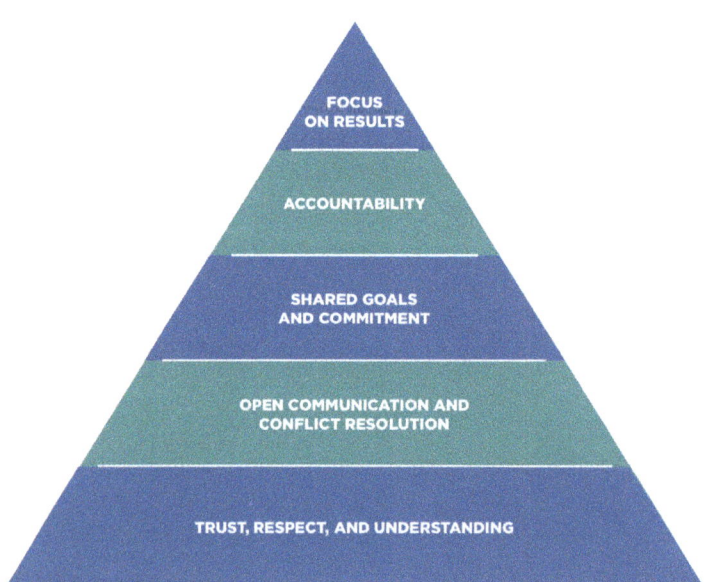

- *Trust, Respect, and Understanding.* Trust is "the confidence among team members that their peers' intentions are good, and that there is no reason to be protective or careful around the group." Trust is built when team members can count on each other, take personal accountability for decisions and actions, and learn from each other. When there is no trust, respect, or understanding, team members will end up jumping to conclusions about the intentions or abilities of others. When respect and understanding are present, team members are much more comfortable asking for help or providing constructive feedback.

- *Open Communication and Conflict Resolution.* Effective teams have open, honest, and direct communication. Healthy debate and disagreement is encouraged; however, the team does not allow individuals to engage in personal attacks or tolerate behind the scenes gossiping and political agendas. This openness fosters an environment where individual group members are comfortable sharing ideas, voicing opinions, and proposing solutions. Most importantly, individuals are not afraid to address controversial topics critical to the team's success.

- *Shared Goals and Commitment.* Great teams establish and gain commitment on shared goals. Shared commitment extends to situations where team members support and are willing to go forward with the group's decision even if they did not support it individually or voted against the idea.

- *Accountability.* Accountability includes a willingness to challenge peers on performance or behaviors that may negatively impact the team's ability to achieve its purpose or goals. WLH advocates that accountability should be high in aligning your focus with goals of the organization, acknowledging when there is an opportunity, asking, "What else can I do?" and achieving the intended results.

The following steps can both underscore and help to imprint the five characteristics across your team:

1. Determine what is new and different with your team. To assess your team's readiness to execute changes, you should first note what is new and different with your team. This should start with an understanding of how much change is taking place. Table 3 outlines the typical team factors and also contains questions to help determine the extent of the changes. In some cases, you will be advised that these things (and other situations) are your own responsibility. If that is the case, you should determine the answers yourself. While this is an exercise that needs to be completed individually, you should consult your team members, manager, and other internal stakeholders, as required, to obtain additional information.

2. Reference the Common Phases of Team Development model to assess your team's development. Once you have determined how your team is being impacted by the organizational changes, it is also important to establish the team's stage of development to determine next steps. For example, how cohesive and productive are the team members as a unit?

The "Common Phases of Team Development" introduced by psychologist Bruce Tuckman in 1965 and revised in 1977 is still a popular model for assessing and guiding teams through organizational change. Use the recommendations provided in the far right column of Table 3 to help your team progress throughout these stages. For example, if they are a newly formed team, you may want them to start by spending more time together in group meetings or different settings where they can get acquainted.

TABLE 3. COMMON PHASES OF TEAM DEVELOPMENT (SOURCE: BRUCE TUCKMAN)

PHASE	DESCRIPTION	RECOMMENDATION
FORMING	In the Forming Stage, team members concentrate on becoming oriented with the tasks they need to do individually, and with one another. Team members are uncommonly polite with each other and avoid serious topics or feelings.	*Focus on clarifying direction and roles. Use teambuilding exercises to help your team move to the next stage.*
STORMING	In the Storming Stage, divergent views are expressed, competition and even conflict can arise. Team members may question responsibilities, rules, and evaluation criteria as they are challenged to bend and mold their ideas, beliefs, and behaviors to suit the team.	*Focus on goals, especially breaking down larger goals into smaller, more manageable ones. Work to establish trust and open communication to move to the next stage.*
NORMING	In the Norming Stage, team members feel more involved and responsible. Team members have developed a level of trust that contributes to the development of team cohesion and the open flow of ideas and solutions between them.	*Focus on how to improve productivity. Help team members challenge each other to think outside the box to move to the next stage.*
PERFORMING	In the Performing Stage, team members are empowered, productive, and collaborative decision makers. Team morale is strong, team loyalty is intense, and team pride in producing superior results is high.	*Continue to work on the development process and results. Make an effort to deepen team members' knowledge and skills. Celebrate successes.*
ADJOURNING / TRANSFORMING	In the Adjourning / Transforming Stage, the team is dissolving or reorganizing for one of two reasons: it has achieved its' purpose successfully, or it has failed badly. In either situation, there may be a feeling of loss or uncertainty as a new group dynamic is established.	*Focus on goals, especially breaking down larger goals into smaller, more manageable ones. Work to establish trust and open communication to move to the next stage.*

Establish/Revise a Vision to Share with Your Team

Effective transition leaders create a vision or picture of success and then inspire their team to buy-in to the necessary change(s) to get there. Each of the steps in this section will help you set the stage. The outcome of the decisions from each step will make up the content for the "jump start meeting" to be held with the team.

In most large organizations, there is a corporate vision. Additionally, divisions or operating units often *Create* their own vision that supports the overall corporate vision. Effective leaders then help others in the organization to see the "big picture," while also understanding what the vision means for them individually in their daily work life.

In his book, *The 8th Habit*, Steve Covey describes the impact of not having a shared vision. In a poll of 23,000 employees drawn from a number of companies and industries, Covey's findings were as follows:

o Only 37 percent said they had a clear understanding of what their organization was trying to achieve and why.

o Only one in five was enthusiastic about their team and organization's goals.

o Only one in five said they had a clear "line of sight" between their tasks and their team and organization's goals.

o Only 15 percent felt their organization fully enabled them to execute key goals.

o Only 20 percent fully trusted the organization they worked for.

Covey then superimposes a very human metaphor over the statistics. He states, "If, say, a soccer team had these same scores, only 4 of the 11 players on the field would know which goal is theirs. Only 2 of 11 would care. Only 2 of the 11 would know what position they play and know exactly what they are supposed to do. And all but 2 players would, in some way, be competing against their own team members rather than the opponent."

A clear vision that resonates with team members has the power to inspire. Effective leaders use vision statements because they can:

o *Create* a picture of what the organization (and team) is striving for.

o Provide clarity on what the organization (and team) is trying to achieve.

o Create enthusiasm and galvanize individuals to move in the same direction.

Use the following points to help you create a clear Team Vision Statement:

- Start with the organization's Mission/Vision and review the language that was used to convey the rationale for change. Ensure this is clear and that you can convincingly convey this information to others.

- Translate this organization-level vision into a more localized vision and mission for the team. Use language that is more meaningful at the local level. What does your team need to achieve?

- Your team members' acceptance of the organization's vision for change is an important foundational guide for their performance. As you develop the Team Vision Statement, think about how you will gain your team members' commitment.

Determine Expectations and Revisit Overall Goals

Effective leaders formulate and convey clear expectations and goals for their teams and provide needed direction that boosts productivity. When a leader does this well, team members are clear on what is expected for success. This prevents team members from "spinning their wheels" on unproductive activities or lower level priorities. Unfortunately, if leaders lack clarity, then individuals will fill the communication and expectation void with their own "best guess." They will assume what the manager or organization is looking for them to accomplish which may not be at all accurate.

The following tips are provided to help you determine expectations and any adjustments to performance needed:

- Formulate behavioral expectations (as specific as possible) for each team member individually and for the team as a whole.

- Think about how the team will need to work together to accomplish their goals. Generate behavioral examples that you would like to see demonstrated and those that you would like to see avoided.

- Establish team priorities.

- Determine specific performance expectations for: required training (e.g. knowledge, systems), maintaining focus on business needs (not being affected by the changes), making any required transitions (e.g., knowledge transfers, customer introductions), making any new connections or alliances required (internal or external), meeting required deadlines, updating specific plans (e.g., customers and accounts), and updating systems or determining new system requirements.

- When creating individual and team goals, draw on your team's organizational performance requirements, the change vision statements, and your personal assessment of how they will need to work together.

- Make sure you follow the S.M.A.R.T. guidelines to Create effective team goals:

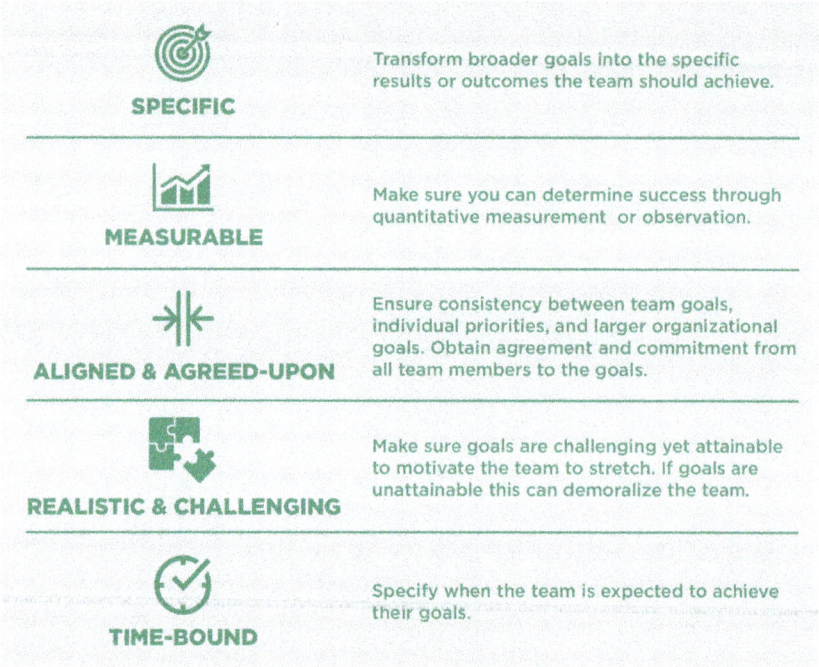

Clarify Roles and Responsibilities for the Team and Team Members

Every organizational change brings uncertainty and potential confusion for individuals. You have an important role as a leader to clarify to your team members any role or team changes resulting from the transition. Additionally, this is a good opportunity to think about whom on the team has unique expertise and experience that can be leveraged with others.

If team members have not changed, make sure they know what is changing and what is staying the same about their individual role and overall team expectations. Alternatively, if you have a new team, ensure that each team member is clear on the following:

> What is their individual role in the team and what are their responsibilities?
>
> What do they need to do as a team?
>
> What is the role of the team in the organization?
>
> What will the organization hold them responsible for?
>
> You should also learn the unique capabilities and attitudes of each team member and determine: Who has specialized knowledge that could benefit the team during the transition?
>
> Who could serve as an internal champion for the change effort?

Proactively assess if any specialized knowledge has been lost due to changes in team composition and make plans for knowledge transfer between old and new team members.

Without shared guidelines for functioning as a team, dysfunction can quickly sprout and grow like unwanted vines around your change program and threaten to strangle your efforts.

The Rules of Engagement typically cover the following topics and themes:

o *Work procedures.* Wherever interdependencies exist between team members, clear procedures should be established for individuals outlining how they will work together, e.g., how to coordinate actions to meet the needs of shared customers. Teams that determine a meeting schedule for physical and virtual team meetings reduce confusion and avoid the challenge of having to find time on the calendar as they move forward. It is always easier to cancel a meeting when no pressing agenda items are present than schedule meetings as needed. Additional ground rules for attendance and participation are also helpful, especially when updating individuals who cannot attend due to other business matters or personal time off. Lastly, a process for determining agenda items reduces confusion and ensures important topics receive the time needed for review and discussion.

o *Communication processes.* Decide what information needs to be shared with whom and how this will occur, e.g., reports, email, or by telephone. Set communication standards around what should or should not be sent in an email. Also, clarify any agreements on times when team members should or should not call each other. Include a process for giving and receiving feedback.

- o *Decision making.* Determine how the team will make decisions, e.g., by consensus, majority, or leadership, and how this may change under different circumstances. Determine norms for recording and communicating decisions and supporting team decisions with others.

- o *Managing conflict.* Gain team commitment to constructively solve conflict by finding win-win solutions. Establish escalation procedures and define when certain approaches should be used: Approach the person *privately*; no gossip or back biting to others. Approach the person with a *peer mediator*; someone trusted by both parties. Approach the person with an *authority figure*; your manager or senior leader, if needed.

Coordinating with Other Stakeholders

As a part of delineating your team's role, you should have a clear understanding of who your team relies on and interacts with. Your team will need knowledge of whom the key internal and external stakeholders are that they will coordinate and communicate with, including everyone they interact with and those affected by the team's activities. This is also important to help identify whom the team needs to inform about important changes, issues, or team progress.

Additionally, you can assist your team by beginning to think about types of information that should be communicated to key stakeholders. There may be information that you want to convey to stakeholders about the change and how it affects your team.

For internal stakeholders, consider informing them of changes in the team's workflow, what they will produce and when, changes in group responsibilities, and/or new collaborative needs. Wherever appropriate, use these updates as an opportunity to reinforce the organization's mission, vision, and goals. Try to use language that mirrors corporate communications and messages about the changes for consistency and to help strengthen commitment throughout the organization. Also, plan on sharing lessons learned and best practices.

If stakeholders are external, consider what they need to know about the organizational changes and what prior communications they may have received from the organization. Whenever appropriate, use the language that mirrors corporate communications and messages about the changes (e.g., language consistent with the organization's mission, vision, and culture).

Establish/Revise Performance Metrics and Monitoring Methods to Reinforce Accountability

Your team should agree on the metrics that will be used to chart individual and team progress. Some metrics will be established by senior leadership; however, high-performing teams practice proactive monitoring to track progress toward goals and then recalibrate. Initial ideas are presented in the "to-do" list below and more guidance on recalibration is provided in Chapter 8. Remember, as the leader you determine the team's culture for accountability by ensuring that metrics are tracked and individuals are held accountable for outcomes.

INITIAL	ONGOING
Determine which tools or reports will be used to assess individual performance.	Make time during team meetings to review the metrics and determine recalibration plans, where needed.
Identify which metrics will be used to chart progress toward the team goals.	Use team meetings as an opportunity to discuss and share best practices for reaching team goals.
Critically examine metrics and data to ensure they are necessary and sufficient for making decisions about progress toward goals.	Examine the team's own practices.
Assign responsibility for tracking metrics.	Reward progress and celebrate success.

Jump Start Your Team!

It is always beneficial for teams to get together, share information, agree on how they will work going forward, develop plans, and address pressing business priorities. This session should also assume a great deal of energy and electricity, as it is the first impression of impending change. The big jump start is essential when a large-scale organizational change is announced.

The phrase, "jump start" will be used throughout this chapter to reference dedicated time for teams to assemble and discuss organizational changes as a group, the impact of the changes to the group, and how the team will work together going forward. Based on your team and their needs, you will need to determine the best approach for a jump start meeting. Factors such as time, number of people, geographical distance separating team members, and other business obligations need to be considered when planning the jump start session. Some organizations will require all teams to go through this exercise, and others will leave it to the team leader's discretion. However, leaders that dedicate one to two days for jump starting their teams will find that the investment in time and energy accelerate the team's work and productivity.

Fully preparing for this meeting will help you have a productive session. In addition to the pre-work you prepared above to establish the vision, expectations, roles/responsibilities, and metrics for your team, you should *Create* a meeting design or detailed agenda for the jump start meeting. The jump start sets the stage for the following goals:

o Impart a clear vision of the team's purpose and how team members will work together.

o Communicate goals and team priorities.

o Articulate the desired outcome of the team's effort.

o Reinforce senior leader expectations and strategic goals.

o Clarify roles and responsibilities.

o Communicate to team members what behaviors you would like to see demonstrated and which behaviors should be avoided.

o Describe the teams' deliverables in concrete terms: reports to produce, plans for implementing or going live with a specific program, sales expectations.

o Work together to develop a detailed plan of action with clear dates, milestones, and responsibilities.

Lasting Impressions

Now that you're all changing, how do you ensure that your enthusiasm seeps through the group? Where do you begin? How do you set the tone?

This section is designed to help you conduct a successful jump start session with your team and to *Create* an environment for open discussion and interactive dialogue. There are specific tips to keep in mind to build trust with your team, develop a team charter, establish rules of engagement, and *Create* action plans.

It's worth stating many times over that high-performing teams are built on trust. Therefore, dedicate time for team members to establish trust and *Create* mutual respect. You can help *Create* a culture of trust and open dialogue by demonstrating tailored leadership behaviors and reinforcing them in others. Talk straight. Speak openly about your beliefs and concerns and show consistency between your words and actions. Be willing to discuss difficult topics and ask for immediate feedback. Demonstrate respect. *Create* a safe environment for open communication by listening, remaining open to different points of view, and showing respect for all team members. For example, respect the confidentiality of private discussions with direct reports.

When there are a lot of new team members, be sure to allow time for individuals to get to know each other. A quick exercise with open-ended questions where team members can share personal background information conveys information about competencies and helps generate mutual respect. These questions could include the following: *How can your past experience help others with the organizational changes? Would you tell us about the types of project teams in which you participated? Tell us about some of the biggest challenges you have faced on other teams and how you dealt with them.*

Create a Team Charter

Remember that balance between formality and fluidity? A team charter could be considered formal in its essence, but the delivery of it can be more informal. By formulating and communicating behavioral expectations and team goals to members, you provide them with a foundation to understand what will be required from the entire team. This is particularly important during times of transition. However, to help the team transform from a group of individuals into a fully functioning and high-performing team that can meet these expectations, they need a shared understanding of their identity as a group and the purpose for which the group serves.

Engage your team in an exercise to Create a Team Charter that consists of specific statements about how the team will succeed. A Team Charter should:

- Be clear and specific about what the team's business is and how it aligns with organizational priorities.

- Include the "boundaries" of the team so individuals know what they are empowered to do and what is outside their scope.

- Be brief enough for team members to keep it in mind.

- Be reflective of the team's agreements regarding communication, collaboration, and coordination.

- Be consistent with the values, beliefs, and philosophy of the organization. For example, a team could include specific behaviors regarding desired business and technical knowledge for team members, teamwork, and collaboration.

Create is the vitality of the 5C's of Transition Leadership®. It underscores how you immerse your team and jump start. In tandem with establishing Rules of Engagement, you have a much greater chance of accelerating performance and results.

Now, Change!
Critical Actions to Create a High-Performing Team

☐ Determine what is new and different with your team.

☐ Understand and assess where your team is along the "Common Phases of Team Development" curve.

☐ Assess your team's commitment to the change.

☐ Establish/revise a vision to share with your team.

☐ Determine expectations and revisit overall goals.

☐ Clarify roles and responsibilities for the team and its members.

☐ Establish/revise performance metrics and monitoring methods to reinforce accountability.

☐ Conduct a team jump start.

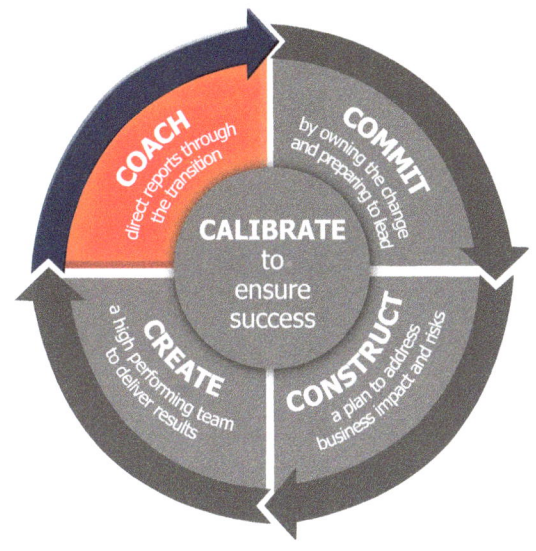

CHAPTER 7

Coach Through Transition

""It is when we are in transition that we are most completely alive."

—William Bridges

Action
COACH direct reports through the transition.

The 30 Percent Success Club Quiz
Why is it important for you to coach direct reports through the transition?

Resistant Mindset
I can continue to coach to performance; there's no need to pay specific attention to transition.

Right Mindset
I provide the energy and perspective needed to help others move through unknown, surprising milestones through transition coaching.

Inside a Change Journey: COACH

The Titanic Treatments team is on Day 2 of their intensive summit. "Fred" has recently experienced career expansion and oversees the largest department at the company. He is not only managing a huge marketing campaign for a new therapy for chronic obstructive pulmonary disease, he's just been hand-picked to be a mentor in the new biotech hub's incubator. All this excitement and activity feeds Fred's career and he is eager to *Coach* the others through transition. He practically lives transition these days!

Remember that when you coach through transition, it will be the individual response that people have to change. The ability to listen and receive feedback is all within *Coach* for the change journey.

Listening effectively and providing feedback are foundational skills necessary to coach effectively. At present, our transition leaders at Titanic Treatments are practicing effective listening: understanding how others feel and see the world, and then giving advice *and* providing comfort in order to solve problems and build relationships more easily.

In turn, the team is using eye contact to keep focused on the speaker and the message, listening to non-verbal cues, keeping an open mind and letting go of preconceived judgments about team members' ability to solve problems or deal with an issue, and most importantly, in today's vast and diverse world, eliminating or reducing barriers that distort listening: bias and cultural myths, hot buttons and buzz words, and physical barriers like fatigue.

In this high-energy exchange, "TNT" is also experiencing a climate for positive feedback, which can be utilized by leaders to reinforce desirable behaviors in the workplace.

Performance-driven coaching does not work during times of change. It lacks the ability to tap into each team member's emotional response to an outside event. Guess what? ...*You're merging!* Guess what? ...*I'm selling off your business!*

These changes elicit a strong, sometimes visceral response in individuals that cannot be fully anticipated. Unlike performance-driven coaching, where continuous development is encouraged (especially when things are smooth sailing), transition coaching requires that you support your team's response to pressing things that are outside of their control. *And outside of your control.* You're responsible for supporting their transition from Point A to Point B.

Within the 5C's, *Coach* is transition coaching. In our parody, many team members of Titanic Treatments may have gaps in knowledge. They may have new customers. How do they learn their customer's profile? And if "Dante" used to work 100 percent of the time remotely and that's all over due to the requirement for more visibility, how can you support him through the new commute, scheduling needs at home, and even the in-person image he will have to project? The leaders have concurred that it will be critical for each of them to spend time with individual direct reports to identify transition gaps and put plans in place to close them. This requires a full-court press of time and effort!

People follow leaders. People don't follow companies. The act of *Coach* in this arena gives leaders skills to stay focused and assess the gaps. It's both understanding the functional and emotional conditions in order to put a plan through so they can go to performance. It requires involvement and commitment. Of the 5C's, *Coach* may be the most misunderstood on the peripheral. While telling, talking, and teaching have a legitimate role in business coaching situations, truly effective transition coaching is a more mutual and interactive process.

Transition coaching is:

o A partnership in which the leader is an advisor, assisting direct reports in the discovery of their own solutions.

o A process to create a working partnership in order to meet business challenges, foster effective customer relationships, drive sales results, and enhance professional development.

o An interactive process that provides feedback and advice on transitional progress and how to navigate roadblocks that hamper change ability.

o A tool to be used by a leader to help others navigate changes successfully.

As transition coach, you are trying to get others on board, committed, and functioning in this new reality. Under "business as usual" conditions, coaching is an important leadership skill for *any* people manager; however, during a major organizational change, coaching individuals through the transition is a critical skill needed for the overall strategic change goals to be achieved. Remember, individuals react emotionally to organizational changes similarly to those of other life-changing events. As a leader of direct reports, determine how the changes are impacting your team and what they need individually for support.

Coaching others through a transition is distinct from everyday management responsibilities where the manager, as coach, provides feedback on performance, capabilities, strengths, and areas for development. You must guide individuals through the transition by helping them with their own reactions to the change and determining how to close any gaps in strategic direction.

The sooner an individual can move through the Transition Cycle, the quicker they can focus on their individual role and become a productive team member. Transition coaching also involves creating an Individual Transition Plan for each direct report.

Utilizing the 5C's, as a transition coach, you help your team members with the following:

- Identify transition challenges they face personally and professionally.

- Understand their strengths and development needs with regard to those challenges.

- Conceptualize and take appropriate action.

- Assess and understand the impact of those actions.

Transition coaching is unique in its focus to guide individuals through the transition process. In Chapter 2, Bridges' "Transition Cycle" was illustrated to describe how people experience the cycle of emotions during change. Your direct report's emotional response, even if a show of modest confusion, is the perfect entryway for your leadership skills. If I were to deliver members of The 30 Percent Success Club to your door—in a massive luxury breathable box wrapped in red, my signature color—they would take the opportunity to fill you in on how they were successful, taking a *whole systems approach*. When it comes to emotion, they understand it's not much ado about nothing—it's much ado about *everything*. If people are reassured that their feelings matter, I guarantee you that they will be motivated to focus more on the task at hand. As a reminder, the 70 Percent Success Club places importance on constant and open communication.

As a transition coach, you will need to help individuals manage their emotions, including their "me issues," build up their confidence, and reinforce their commitment to the transition. Even those individuals who embrace change may experience corollary emotions that are decidedly unpleasant—in particular, the feeling of being overwhelmed.

For best results, it is recommended that transition coaching take place during one-on-one meetings between the leader and the direct report. The meetings can be face-to-face or via teleconference.

There is no specific guideline for how long the process should take to complete, though it can often be completed in less than two hours. More important than timing, however, is to ensure that each step is done well. The accurate identification of transition challenges, strengths, and potential development needs is necessary for producing a fantastic coaching outcome.

A bulletproof strategy to follow for all coaching sessions is to take the time to plan what you hope to accomplish in each meeting. Review any relevant notes from past meetings. If you treat these sessions in a serious fashion, you will encourage those you coach to do the same and they will be more productive. Also, during your first session with a direct report, you can suggest that they prepare for subsequent meetings by reviewing the topics and writing a few notes about their goals in advance.

Six primary steps involved in effective transition coaching will ensure your resounding success:

Step 1. Establish or renew a working relationship.

The purpose of this step is to define the nature of the coaching relationship between you and your direct report. In cases where you both have little or no experience with one another, this step will take longer than when substantial familiarity does exist. In this step, you and your direct report should:

o Introduce yourselves and share something from your background and experience. (In cases where the leader and direct report know each other well, this can be skipped.)

- Share a few general expectations, reactions, and concerns about the transition.
- Describe the commitment to the transition process and to the organization overall.
- Set ground rules for any follow-up discussions (time, location, and schedule): Establish an open and collegial atmosphere. Emphasize your coaching commitment. Reinforce any key messages regarding the strategic direction and business priorities.

Step 2. Identify transition challenges.

In this step, the goal is to assist your direct report with identifying specific challenges they feel due to the change in strategy. Change often poses organizational and personal challenges. You should encourage the exploration of both.

- Ask open-ended questions such as, "How do you feel about the role?"
- Avoid closed-ended questions, i.e., a question that can be answered with either a "yes" or "no" reply.
- Be willing to share some of your own feelings about the change—both positive and negative.
- Discuss specific transition tasks and how they will be addressed (e.g., any training requirements or knowledge transfers with other colleagues).
- Reach an agreement on the two or three most pressing challenges.
- Summarize the conversation to gain clarity for yourself and for your direct report.

As a team leader, you should have made a few personal assessments of each direct report and how they have been managing the transition in general. For example: *What is their overall "readiness" to perform new required duties? Do they understand role requirements? Are they accepting the changes? Do they believe in the approach or are they resistant to the transition? Are they managing the transition well or do they seem overwhelmed? Are they showing signs of being a potential retention risk?*

Use the personal assessment you created for your direct report to examine the challenges that were initially discussed with you. Then gently challenge them if you think there may be other issues to be considered.

Step 3. Identify strengths and development needs.

After a mutual agreement on the major challenges is reached, move on to assist your direct report with identifying individual strengths and developmental needs vis-à-vis the change. The goal in this step is to help your direct report explore the gap between their current level of skill or ability and think about what it will take to close any gaps.

Major transition is not the time for long-term development planning (as tempting as it may be). Rather, the focus should be on assisting the direct report to explore practical methods for them to implement and be successful, e.g., managing immediate transition issues. Ask about current strengths they may have to successfully engage in the change and development capabilities they may need to meet current challenges. Once you reach consensus on both their strengths and development needs, summarize and seek clarification often.

Step 4. Set transition change goals and timelines.

In this step, you should help the direct report establish a set of S.M.A.R.T. (Specific, Measurable, Attainable, Realistic, and Time-Specific) goals to leverage their strengths, close short-term skill or learning gaps, and adopt strategies to minimize the impact of any longer-term development needs.

For example, your direct report may have identified "impatience" as a weakness that becomes more prominent during times of change or other stressful situations. In this step, your aim would be to help the direct report develop a goal pertaining to how to deal and work with their impatience.

o Ask your direct report to explore how their strengths and weaknesses relate to each of the transition challenges identified in Step 2.

o Develop a goal statement for each transition challenge. This should state how they would anticipate applying strength or working around a weakness to meet that challenge.

o Reach agreement and record each goal statement.

o Help your direct report to be specific about their strengths and weaknesses.

o Summarize and seek clarification often.

Step 5: Develop an Individual Transition Plan.

Next, you should help your direct report develop an Individual Transition Plan to meet each of the transition change goals they set in Step 4. The plan should detail how they will reach each goal and it should be as specific as possible. To encourage specificity, ask your direct report how they can capitalize on their strengths and compensate for their weaknesses to reach their goals.

- Assist with brainstorming alternative actions for each change challenge.
- Encourage the individual to talk about sources of help or support that they might call upon during the transition.
- Reach agreement with your direct report on a final plan and the timing to monitor progress.
- Ensure that the plan is recorded for future review.

Step 6: Evaluate and recalibrate Individual Transition Plan.

The plan developed in Step 5 should contain regular review dates. In this step, the goal is to meet at a regularly scheduled time with your direct report and review ongoing progress of their Individual Transition Plan.

- Record future follow-up sessions in your calendar.
- Use ongoing conversations as an opportunity to check-in on transition plans.
- Celebrate success.
- Treat shortfalls as opportunities for learning.
- Direct the individual to longer-term development opportunities, as appropriate.
- Help your direct report recalibrate their action plan, as necessary.

Retention Risk and the Potential Loss of Critical Talent

Team member retention is a "special" category of business risk, especially during times of change.

Many factors contribute to employee retention and often these factors become more apparent during large-scale change initiatives. While some employees will always switch companies for more pay, compensation does not turn out to be a significant or primary reason why most high performers decide to stay or leave. Other factors predict or drive an employee's decision to stay with a company. Under the category that would be considered "manager-employee relationship," factors such as positive work environment, coaching and supervision, performance management, training and career advancement, and rewards/recognition are included. During times of change, it is important to evaluate your role in contributing to a solid manager-employee relationship.

As you assess each of your direct reports during the large-scale change initiative, it is important to determine if there are individuals at risk of leaving the organization. For example, during a merger/integration, employees face the potential of losing their jobs and become anxious about the announced change well before restructuring plans are announced. In addition, the prospect of a new boss, new co-workers, new location, and new responsibility creates a great deal of uncertainty.

Time and again, top talent may be the first to leave even before final plans are put in place. What is going on within your organization and with your team that would accelerate the loss of top talent?

Understand how the transition will impact each individual and a potential desire to leave the organization. Here are a few critical areas to think about and suggestions to reduce retention risk:

Look for the warning signs from a normally positive and productive team member that might suggest they are considering leaving:

o Missing deadlines or cancelling appointments.

o Working only required hours, arriving late or leaving early.

o Only doing the minimum.

o Taking unscheduled vacation or sick days.

o Avoiding or turning down assignments.

- Arguing more than usual or more passionately about issues.
- Complaining or gossiping about the boss, co-workers, or the company.
- Acquiescing when they normally would be more challenging.
- Shutting down or failing to participate.

Meet with team members you suspect may be at risk of leaving to reopen communication, identify needs, and address problem areas. Talking with them and focusing on solutions can be a powerful re-recruitment intervention:

- Ask them what is going well and what is not going well.
- Don't confront the symptoms.
- Do question, listen, and explore in-depth.
- Emphasize your commitment to the team member.
- Focus on their positive goals.
- Find creative ways to resolve differences.
- Agree on a mutual plan of action and follow-up on commitments.
- Clarify their responsibility for next steps.

Feedback—Give and Take!

Effective feedback increases insight and motivates action. In other words, feedback provides information that helps a direct report perform beyond historical results.

To ensure feedback is constructive and reduces resistance, be clear about what did or didn't meet expectations, why it did or didn't meet expectations, and what the impact is on the team and/or the organization.

When providing feedback, ask yourself the following questions to ensure your comments meet the requirements of positive and constructive feedback: *Am I giving this feedback to be helpful? Am I giving feedback soon after the incident or just prior to the next similar event? Have I considered how I would feel as the recipient of this feedback? Do I use non-judgmental language when delivering feedback? Am I using concrete examples and observations? Do I focus on the work being reviewed rather than making personal judgments? Am I clearly illustrating the benefits of making required changes? Do I provide follow-up feedback when appropriate? Do I provide positive reinforcement when behavior has changed? Am I being fair, e.g., providing feedback on something they have no power to change?*

Everyone or No One—Empathy

Using empathy involves recognizing and acknowledging the feelings of others. When people express strong emotions (happiness, embarrassment, anger, frustration), your empathetic response conveys sympathy and understanding which facilitates discussion and builds trust. Empathy can also be helpful for reducing conflict and helping others to see common goals, so it is worth considering these tips for employing empathy:

- Use empathy to get at feelings in a non-threatening way. Some people have a hard time discussing feelings, which can get in the way of moving forward to address a problem or issue.

- Paraphrase and play back what you hear. Paraphrasing allows the person to hear what they are expressing and re-examine it. This is more effective than saying, "You shouldn't feel that way."

- Do not take a position. Empathy does not imply agreement with, sharing or condoning the feeling; it just says that you understand.

- Avoid "hot button" words to describe feelings, e.g., furious, agitated, depressed, and use words that allow the person to continue to explain or clarify, e.g., annoyed, upset, concerned, disappointed.

- Don't worry about identifying the feeling incorrectly. The point you want to convey is that you are trying to understand the full message.

- Pause after using empathy; let them respond. Do not immediately follow with advice, your solution, or a question about what they will do. If you don't allow them time to process the feeling and respond to your paraphrase, the sincerity of your message is diluted.

Of the 5C's, *Coach* is dynamic and actionable (thus, the many tips and tricks!). In essence, transition coaching is very much hands-on, immediate, and focused on specific needs within a partnership. It is a mutual and interactive process that makes all the difference in a new reality where everyone thrives and your organization excels and innovates.

Now, Change!
Critical Actions to Coach
Direct Reports through Transition

☐ Learn the fundamentals of transition coaching.

☐ Follow the transition coaching process guidelines.

☐ Address retention risks and the potential loss of critical talent.

☐ Assess your areas of strength and weakness as a coach.

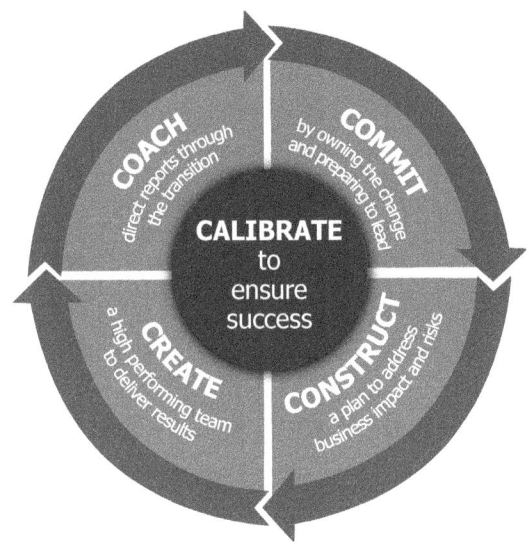

CHAPTER 8

Establish Metrics and Milestones

"Effective leadership is putting first things first. Effective management is discipline, carrying it out."

—Stephen Covey

Action
CALIBRATE to ensure success.

The 30 Percent Success Club Quiz
Why is it important for you to examine your commitments and ability to lead?

Resistant Mindset
I don't have time to measure results.

Right Mindset
I have time to create a process for ongoing review and recalibration of change efforts to ensure success.

Inside a Change Journey: CALIBRATE

After two days of learning the 5C's of Transition Leadership, the 150 participants at Titanic Treatments are being tested today on their ability to course-correct. It may be instinctual to learn a new process or technology and then use it according to a transition plan. It may not be an "automatic" activity to monitor results, contemplate adjustments, and make those adjustments in order to meet final goals. *Calibrate* makes up these actions and ensures success.

Common questions are floating about the room regarding measures and tracking: "If you are paying attention to your people who completed the transition plan, how do you know if they are applying the same care to the plan without micro-managing?" "Are they working through the process?" "What measures should you be putting in place?" "Why should you?"

Change is constantly occurring, even at a micro-level, so it is valuable to calibrate and recalibrate continuously. Since you never know what micro-changes may be impacting your overall success, keep your eyes open.

In the rush to stand out and forge herculean improvements, this team's transition leader is reminded not to be so blind to the fundamentals of the training that the reasons for change are forgotten.

"Simone" experienced this before at her previous employer, a competing biotech giant. Her own transition leader set the revenue-generating stage in the beginning with diamonds in his eyes. Then, when the training got underway, he stopped communicating the fundamentals and got lost in the process, often showing his own irritation when her team members didn't just assume things. They worked from instinct and their own expertise in order to get the change program done, but there had been no training on measurement and tracking. When the program collapsed into results that were mediocre at best, headcount was chopped.

Simone was thrilled to receive the type of training that would prevent such a catastrophe. She couldn't be affected by a few of the other senior leaders yawning and barely existing, like zombies, at her table.

As the Titanic Treatment leaders rounded up the intensive three-day summit, they agreed to a common set of metrics and process to communicate with each other on their progress. Sharing lessons learned would undoubtedly help each of them and the organization as a whole.

Calibration is often forgotten but critically important. As long as you continue to wake up with the following question, your change program will continue to evolve: "I put this plan in place, but how do I need to fix it?" Simply put, if you put someone on new medication, you have to check its effectiveness, continuously tweak dosage and sometimes even consider an alternative prescription due to its side effects. Organizationally, people announce the change, *one and done*, and "Oh, we're good!" They think everything is going to work well. It just doesn't.

Calibration functions on multiple levels, but for the leader level, you need to see that the transition plans are working. Are they tracking? Are they meeting objectives? Making sure to course-correct early so it doesn't cost so much? Organizations do not calibrate. They spend more time invested on this first plush announcement and they're not tracking.

If you're building a house, you're not just meeting with the architect and saying, "Great plan!" You're checking to see how it's going. You see the blueprints, visit during framing, see the big reveal, and then go back through the house with blue tape for tweaks. The "blue tape" phase is literally calibration. The house is done, but it's not quite right.

Calibration should be part of the way in which you run the business and lead your teams. Prior chapters focused on helping team leaders develop a transition plan to successfully implement the proposed changes with their team. If team leaders followed the various steps and addressed the multiple considerations associated with implementing a change effort provided in the previous chapters, then they will have already addressed a common cause of change failure: inadequate planning. Without a structured process for creating a transition plan, there can be the tendency to miss critical business risks or underestimate the impact of change on the team and individual direct reports.

Another common cause of change failure occurs when leaders try to rush the adoption of change. This can cause negative results that include inconsistent implementation and increased resistance. Instead, managers should keep a key principle in mind: Large-scale change implementation is a marathon and not a sprint.

Therefore, proper transition planning should include specific strategies for sustaining efforts over time and tracking overall progress. Calibration is the method and the process for ensuring this takes place. Calibration involves tracking progress, at specified intervals with agreed upon metrics, and making needed adjustments.

Calibration is essential for keeping transition plans on track to meet intended goals. Calibration involves creating metrics that reinforce goals and sending clear messages about accountability for results. It also involves creating an ongoing process for monitoring, communicating, and adjusting the transition plans based on these metrics to keep everyone on the same page and moving forward together.

When calibration is done well, it serves as an early warning system that enables course correction before an issue becomes a major problem. Good calibration will prevent a team from fighting fire drill after fire drill, make the process of change smoother, and boost the likelihood of meeting final change goals.

Establishing and maintaining a calibration process with a schedule for examining progress and adjusting actions also helps reinforce the long-term attention and efforts needed to reach large-scale change goals.

As a manager, you are ultimately responsible for the productivity of your team. You already use metrics to track and gauge your team's performance, and some of these will be equally applicable for tracking progress toward change goals. However, you should examine existing metrics to see if they will be sufficient for tracking progress toward change goals and create additional ones if they are needed now. Additional metrics may provide a more complete picture of your team's growth and improvements, better demonstrate the effectiveness of the changes, and/or provide an improved early warning system of potential problems.

Many of the metrics you should use for tracking change will be determined by the deliverables your team is responsible for producing and the goals of the overall change effort. If you are unclear on which metrics to use to track your team's deliverables, you can consult with your manager or team members for the reports and systems that will provide the most vital information.

For metrics that demonstrate the effectiveness of individual and team transitions, or adoption of the change, consider using a range of both qualitative and quantitative metrics. Qualitative data may include measures of employees' attitudes. *How have they changed since the transition was announced? Did they improve after specific actions (e.g., a focus group that allowed them to air any issues, or a town meeting to address their concerns)?* Quantitative data may include measures such as turnover rates, productivity rates, and other employee satisfaction benchmarks or surveys to determine the effectiveness of communication initiatives.

Calibration team meetings should serve a few key purposes including sharing successes, updating each other on important lessons learned, and determining what course corrections are required. As a result, it is important to continuously update the team's transition plan. Ensure responsibility is clear for any new action items and that milestones are established and recorded in the plan to maintain clarity on the path forward.

Calibration meetings should also provide an opportunity to share what is and is not working to provide praise where it is due and to celebrate success. At the calibration meetings, allow people to describe their successes, lessons learned, disappointments, and surprises. Encourage suggestions for how to improve future implementation efforts, for both your team and other teams. This can promote organizational learning about successful change management. Make sure to focus on what is working and to build upon any successes. Building off of early wins will create positive momentum and a climate of focusing on what is working versus what is not. Share stories of success with senior management because early successes can help sustain individuals' engagement in the transition (throughout the organization).

The schedule for reporting established metrics is typically pre-determined by your organization and any business requirements. However, in the Transition Plan, it is important to re-examine when and how frequently the team should monitor these and other metrics developed to track change goals. For example, many new managers develop thirty-, sixty-, and ninety-day action plans to track their success. This can also be useful for tracking the success of change implementation efforts with your team. For example, the following sample objectives can be used for the first ninety days:

o Understand current opportunities and challenges.

o Successfully manage all personal transition issues.

o Team members accept vision for the future.

o The team is making collective progress managing the transition.

Thirty-, Sixty-, Ninety-Day Plan

The following table can help you formulate a basic action plan. Replace the text using the sample questions and suggestions.

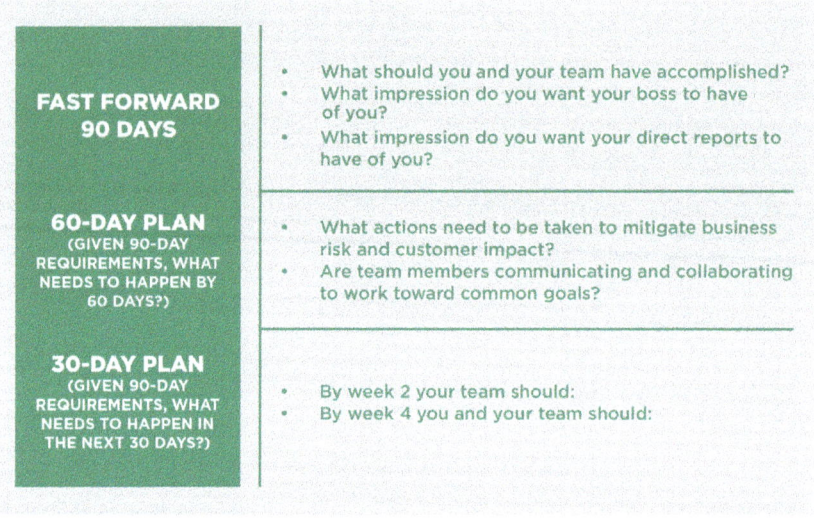

FAST FORWARD 90 DAYS	• What should you and your team have accomplished? • What impression do you want your boss to have of you? • What impression do you want your direct reports to have of you?
60-DAY PLAN (GIVEN 90-DAY REQUIREMENTS, WHAT NEEDS TO HAPPEN BY 60 DAYS?)	• What actions need to be taken to mitigate business risk and customer impact? • Are team members communicating and collaborating to work toward common goals?
30-DAY PLAN (GIVEN 90-DAY REQUIREMENTS, WHAT NEEDS TO HAPPEN IN THE NEXT 30 DAYS?)	• By week 2 your team should: • By week 4 you and your team should:

o Regularly review progress toward transition goals using established metrics to ensure milestones and deadlines are met:

- Create a schedule of team meetings when metrics will be reviewed and options will be discussed for maintaining progress or recalibrating efforts.

- Determine who will be responsible for tracking and reporting metric data and how they will communicate these findings to the team (and to other stakeholders, as required).

o Recalibrate efforts when goals are not being met:

- Track progress toward goals to enable course corrections *before* it is too late. Have a process for communicating important feedback between meetings

- Determine actions that can be taken to improve outcomes. Create action items and assign responsibility. Follow-up on these diligently.

o Communicate progress, setbacks, and proposed solutions to key stakeholders to keep them in the loop and demonstrate proactivity:

- This helps publicly reward your team members and holds them responsible for outcomes.

- This helps communicate issues to others outside the control of your team so they can be promptly addressed.

Finally, calibration meetings can represent an important method of making your team members feel like they "have a voice" and that their concerns are being heard and considered. This will help them get on board with the changes, progress through the transition phases described above, boost loyalty and productivity, and help them feel like a valued member of the team and the organization.

If the calibration meeting is not an appropriate forum for this, then create alternate ways for people to communicate opinions, experiences, and reactions to change or decisions being made at the team level. This can be done through an e-mail site, a technical support group, focus groups, or through a survey. Respond to your direct reports as much as you are able. For example, offer interim accommodations to concerns if you are able to provide them.

Establishing effective two-way communication can also help organizational leaders learn about issues or concerns before they become formal grievances or even lawsuits.

In closing, always be communicating to ensure coordination and sustained change efforts. During calibration meetings, leaders should also determine what information should to be shared with these stakeholders related to overall progress, plan updates, and lessons learned. Regular ongoing communications from your team helps others avoid surprises and engage in early course corrections as well, if required. It also reinforces a culture of information sharing and continuous learning.

Now, Change!
Critical Actions to Calibrate to Achieve Success

- ☐ Determine specific metrics, milestones, and responsibilities for tracking progress.
- ☐ Create a process for ongoing review and recalibration of change efforts to ensure success.
- ☐ Communicate to ensure coordination and sustained change efforts.

OUT OF THE WILD

Now, Change! (Complete Your Transition Plan)

> "You will never do anything in this world without courage. It is the greatest quality of the mind next to honor."
>
> —Aristotle

You cannot rush through this wild and wondrous process of change and transition leadership. The world is consumed with micro learning and as a result, people think they read articles on Google and become "experts." Keeping a search engine burning and buzzing is not the courageous behavior of a 30 Percent Success Club member.

People are human beings—feeling, thinking, working, and changing. When you change their world and move their cheese, not all will adapt! You have early adopters, but perhaps three-fourths of people are resisters. Unless you're intentional about working with them, you are not going to get results.

As a transition leader, you may not be tasked with eradicating the world's foremost challenges, while also undergoing a 90-day change initiative and coaching your team through. However, you took your education and career responsibilities seriously enough in order to command a leadership seat. You instinctually know that change happens. Your professional life continues breathing by the world's lungs of change across every industry. You will master the transition(s), which means that you've successfully led your people through the cave beneath a mountain range despite rain and a few sore attitudes. With such a monumental accomplishment, you positively transform. Your team transforms. Your company transforms. The industry evolves. The world expands its lungs.

The following tools were selected specifically to support you as you navigate change and transition. These tools are taken directly from the 5C's of Transition

Leadership® program, and I hope you find them extremely useful in your new reality. That reality promises to be wildly fulfilling now that you will *Change and Thrive* with the vital ability to:

o   Assess and address personal needs and gaps related to organizational change.

o   Determine how the change impacts the business and make plans to ensure performance goals are met, while also addressing potential business risks.

o   Translate the strategic change effort and take steps to create a high-performing team.

o   Assess and coach each direct report's challenges and personal commitment to the organizational change.

o   Establish metrics and milestones for success.

TRANSITION PLAN:
COMMIT BY OWNING THE CHANGE AND PREPARING TO LEAD

Personal Transition Plan **Commit by Owning the Change and Preparing to Lead**	
Any actions to improve Personal Change Readiness	
Actions for Communicating the Business Case for Change (in your own words)	
Actions to address Learning Gaps	

Personal Commitments	
As a transition change leader, I must demonstrate the following behaviors:	
During the next 90 days, I will measure my own success by:	
My commitment(s) to "walk the talk" include:	

TRANSITION PLAN:
CONSTRUCT A PLAN TO ADDRESS BUSINESS IMPACT AND RISKS

Use this worksheet to record the steps you will take to "Construct a plan to address business impact and risks."	
Actions needed to maintain focus during times of change	
Actions needed to address the most important business risks for me to address	
Communications to others regarding risk mitigation plans	

TRANSITION PLAN: CREATE A HIGH PERFORMING TEAM

Use this worksheet to note the actions required to "Create a High Performing Team."	
Formulate leadership expectations that will be important to share with your team	
Determine how to leverage individuals on the team to help others act as experts	
Outline actions to prepare for upcoming Jump Start Meeting: o Develop an Agenda o Select a date and location o Draft an initial Team Charter o Prepare materials o Update Manager on plans	

TRANSITION PLAN: COACH OTHERS THROUGH THE TRANSITION

	Include in your Transition Plan actions related to "Coach Others Through the Transition."
Determine steps to identify individual team members' transition challenges	
Establish meetings to discuss how best to close any individual transition gaps	
Determine if there are any retention risks and develop a plan to re-recruit	
Take action to improve your own transition coaching capabilities	

TRANSITION PLAN:
CALIBRATE TO ENSURE SUCCESS

Include in your Transition Plan actions required to "Calibrate to Ensure Success"	
What are some key messages that I want to communicate to my team?	
To calibrate my transition plan, I will: o Establish milestones o Set measurements for success o Calendar any meetings / calls o Report progress to my manager	

About the Author

Wendy L. Heckelman, Ph.D., president and founder of WLH Consulting, Inc. has more than 28 years of experience working with Fortune 100 clients in the areas of pharmaceuticals, animal health care, consumer health care, biotech, financial services, distribution services, international non-profit organizations, and growing entrepreneurial companies.

Clients consistently rely on Wendy to guide them through complex and large-scale projects related to strategic planning and execution. Her expertise centers on helping leaders refine and focus their strategies to maximize internal core capabilities, while also addressing marketplace challenges. Additionally, Wendy partners with clients to define and reinforce cultural tenets as a driver for change and effectiveness. WLH has been a strategic partner in multiple merger integration projects, as well as numerous large-scale expansions and organizational restructurings.

As a skilled facilitator of executive-level programs, Wendy has worked with leadership groups in over 25 countries throughout Europe, Latin America, and Asia. She also serves as an executive coach to many senior and executive leaders. Some of her top clients come from Pfizer, Boehringer-Ingelheim, Bristol-Meyers Squibb, Astra Zeneca, Johnson and Johnson, Regeneron, Zoetis, Akcea, Acorda Therapeutics, Kaiser Permanente, Avon, Allergan, and Sunovion.

Wendy has presented her work at several national conferences including the Healthcare Businesswomen's Association (HBA), Life Sciences and Educators Network (LTEN), Organizational Development Network, Society for Human Resource Professionals, Pharma Congress, and the International Quality and Productivity Center.

Wendy holds M.S. and Ph.D. degrees in Organizational Psychology from Columbia University, and a Master's in Education in Counseling from Columbia. She serves as South East Regional President of Corporate Partnerships for the Healthcare Businesswomen's Association (HBA). She is on the advisory board of the Southeast Medical Device Association and the Alliance Theatre.

Change and Thrive: A Modern Approach to Change Leadership is Wendy's debut book.

References

Ackerman Anderson, L. & Anderson, D. (2002). The Ten Most Common Mistakes in Leading Transformational Change. Retrieved from http://changeleadersnetwork.com/free-resources/ten-common-mistakes-in-leading-transformation.

Arnold, Paul. "The 5 Greatest Examples of Change Management in Business History." Chartered Management Institute. July 20, 2015. https://www.managers.org.uk/insights/news/2015/july/the-5-greatest-examples-of-change-management-in-business-history.

Bridges, William. *Managing Transitions, 25th anniversary edition: Making the Most of Change*. New York, New York: De Capo Lifelong Books: 2017.

Brown, Brené. *Dare to Lead*. New York, New York: Random House, 2018.

Chaudron, D. (2003). The Nine Pitfalls of Organizational Change. Retrieved from: http://www.organizedchange.com/ninepitfallsoforganizationalchange.htm

Christensen, Clayton. *The Innovator's Dilemma*. New York, New York: HarperBusiness, 2011.

Covey, S. *The 8th Habit: From Effectiveness to Greatness*. New York, New York: Free Press, 2002.

Deloitte US Center for the Edge
https://www2.deloitte.com/us/en/pages/center-for-the-edge/solutions/about-center-for-the-edge.html

Drucker, Peter. *The Effective Executive*. New York, New York: HarperBusiness, 2006.

Grenny, Joseph. *Influencer: The New Science of Leading Change, Second Edition*. New York, New York: McGraw-Hill, May 2013.

Herper, Matthew. "New York City Puts Up $100 Million To Create A Biotech Hub." *Forbes*. January 23, 2018.

https://www.forbes.com/sites/matthewherper/2018/01/23/new-york-puts-up-100-million-asks-for-plans-for-a-biotech-hub/#7594c12a392c.

Holman, P., Devane, T., Cady, S. (Eds.) (2007). *The Change Handbook: The Definitive Resource on Today's Best Methods for Engaging Whole Systems.* Berrett-Koehler Publishers, Inc.: San Francisco, CA

Keller, S. Aiken, C. (Aug. 14, 2000). The Inconvenient Truth About Change Management. Retrieved from: http://www.mckinsey.com/App_Media/Reports/Financial_Services/The_Inconvenient_Truth_About_Change_Management.pdf

Kotter, John. *Leading Change.* Boston, Massachusetts: *Harvard Business Review,* 2012.

Kotter, John. Leading Change: Why Transformation Efforts Fail. *Harvard Business Review, March-April,* 1995, pp. 59-67.

Kouzes, Jim and Posner, Barry, The Leadership Challenge (5th Edition), Jossey-Bass: New York, NY.

Lencioni, P. (2002). The Five Dysfunctions of a Team. Jossey-Bass: San Francisco, CA. (pg. 195).

McKinsey & Company. "Disruption, friction, and change: The hallmarks of a true transformation." *McKinsey Quarterly.* October 2017. https://www.mckinsey.com/business-functions/rts/our-insights/disruption-friction-and-change-the-hallmarks-of-a-true-transformation

Meinert, D. (2012). Wings of change. *HR Magazine, November,* pp. 30-36.

Palmer, J. Change Management In Practice: Why Does Change Fail? Retrieved from: http://www.articledashboard.com/Article/Change-Management-In-Practice-Why-Does-Change-Fail/35180

Schein, Edgar. *Organizational Culture and Leadership, 5th Edition (The Jossey-Bass Business & Management Series).* New York, New York: Wiley, December 2016.

Shoemaker, Paul. "6 Habits of True Strategic Thinkers," *Inc.,* March 20, 2012.

Stanier, Michael Bungay. *The Coaching Habit: Say Less, Ask More & Change the Way You Lead Forever.* Toronto, Canada: Box of Crayons Press. February 2016.

Thompson Jr., LeRoy, *Mastering the Challenges of Change: Strategies for Each Stage in Your Organization's Life Cycle.* New York: AMACOM. 1994.

Tuckman, B. W., & Jensen, M. A. C. (1977). Stages of small-group development revisited. *Group & Organization Studies, 2*(4), 419-427.

Yueh, Linda. "Nokia, Apple and Creative Destruction." *BBC.com.* May 1, 2014. https://www.bbc.com/news/business-27238877.

Zenger, Jack. "Individual Leadership Development Versus A Company's Leadership Development." *Forbes.* January 13, 2019.
https://www.forbes.com/sites/jackzenger/2019/01/13/individual-leadership-development-versus-a-companys-leadership-development/#115f6cf177dc